PREACHING ON
PENTECOST
And Christian Unity

Thirty outstanding sermons dealing with the theme of
Pentecost and the ecumenical movement.

Edited by

ALTON M. MOTTER

FORTh

Phila

DEDICATION

This book is affectionately dedicated to those Christian leaders who have challenged my heart and mind by the high quality of their leadership in the life and work of the church ecumenical.

ALTON M. MOTTER

PREFACE

There is a growing feeling that Pentecost deserves a more significant observance in the life of the church. This motivation led the publishers to request a collection of sermons* which would deal basically with the experience of Pentecost and which would also relate that experience to developments in the modern movement toward greater Christian unity.

An increasing number of scholars have long testified to the ecumenical overtones of Pentecost. It has seemed appropriate, therefore, for the presidents of the World Council of Churches to issue their annual "message" to the millions of members of the Council's 209 member church bodies on this day.

Readers will find in this volume a collection of significant insights dealing with the spiritual rootage of the ecumenical movement. This is especially true for the sermons of Bridston, Nelson, Osborn, Norgren, Northcott, Cate, Miller, and Payne.

Other writers like Carlson, Bergendoff, and Smith wrestle with some of the more specific theological questions related to the movement.

Many readers will welcome both the constructive spirit and content of the plea for greater Protestant-Catholic understanding by Catholic writers, Gannon and McCorry.

The largest number of sermons come within the category of

* Previous volumes by the same editor and publishers include *Preaching the Resurrection* (1959); *Preaching the Nativity* (1961); and *Preaching the Passion* (1963).

biblical preaching and include sermons written by Marty, Osborn, Rogness, Robinson, Read, Haselden, Herbster, Robinson, Sockman, Dahlberg, Hoffmann, and Visser 't Hooft. Some of these are expository while others are topical in style.

The sermon by Cavert, because of its exceedingly valuable interpretation of the nature of the church which resulted from Pentecost, may be considered by many to be one of the most helpful sermons in the volume.

Other readers will find the way Littell relates his theme to the sociological conditions of modern society and the thesis of McCracken upon the urgency for reaching the non-Christian world, unusually helpful contributions.

The writers come from a dozen different Christian traditions including the Roman Catholic. Two hail from England. All have contributed to our understanding of what happened on that first day of Pentecost in the Christian era when the church was both born and baptized by the Holy Spirit and the way that same Spirit seeks to guide the church today.

Alton M. Motter

Minneapolis, Minnesota

CONTENTS

PREACHING ON PENTECOST

by MARKUS BARTH

Pittsburgh Theological Seminary,
Pittsburgh, Pa.

ACTS 2:1-40

Let all be warned of what is to follow. I am not trying to give a prescription, solution, or example of how a sermon on Acts 2 should look. I know what the listener expects from the preacher: "Lord, we would see Jesus!" It is the sacred duty of a preacher to show forth Jesus and to preach the gospel. But today I have to act against my own conviction and instruction regarding the essence and purpose of a sermon. The Geneva gown I am wearing is after all not a prophetic mantle like Elijah's; neither is it a clerical cassock, implying the obligation to a specific type of preaching. It is an academic garb, and in academical fashion I intend to say a few words on the act of preaching itself, based on the text we have heard from Acts.

It may be doubted whether Martin Dibelius and some of his followers are right who consider the sermons in Acts a-historical and explain them as mere makeshifts of Luke who, presumably, wanted to give his readers examples of how to preach in different situations. We may rather assume that, precisely because a

1

speech like Peter's Pentecostal address has its roots in authentic history, it also may have been remembered and reproduced by Luke as a precedent for all exposed to the task and trial of preaching.

Therefore we ask today, what is preaching in the light of this sermon?

We answer first with a few negatives: It is not an act of looking backward, reflecting on a god of the past. It does not presuppose that with Jesus Christ's ascension revelation is over, and the book of God's mighty acts is closed. It does not convey the impression of any of the convulsions by which we modern preachers attempt to make relevant, to communicate, or to apply the "meaning" of bygone stories and doctrines. Absent is the spell of the magician who pulls mice out of his old hat; also there is no trace of underlying boredom. Peter does not speak of a god who is dead or retired, and he does not advertise himself by announcing that he, finally, will make the doctrinal and philosophical deductions necessary in order to be "honest to God" before contemporary listeners.

But he speaks very much of the present. Consider the frame and occasion of his speech.

Here is a room or court belonging to Israel's Temple. Peter and his listeners do not disdain the opportunity given by insitutional religion. A festival with agricultural or historical background (beginning of harvest or giving of the law) is being celebrated. For us, the virtual residue of nature-religion or the possible triumph of legalistic religion in that festival are reasons to lift some eyebrows: Can a Christian participate in such a

2

feast? At any rate, Peter does participate! Organized religion is no excuse for him to be blind to God's work in the temple, and to be mute. It cannot prevent God from being present and showing his presence in action.

Next: Peter is involved in a group experience. He does not tell of his own calling, conversion, communion, but he speaks of the things that have happened on that very day, to the disciples first and then to the crowds when those given the Spirit began to "sound off" publicly. The experiences of the smaller and the larger group did certainly include those of all individuals present; but Luke's description of the event and the sermon puts primary emphasis upon the whole (Mediterranean) world represented by those assembled, on the promise of the Spirit to all flesh, on Jesus Christ's dominion over all enemies (vss. 7-11, 17, 34-35). And only in conclusion special references are made to "every one of you" and to personal salvation "from this crooked generation" (vss. 21, 38, 40). The personal moments of inspiration, decision, faith are certainly not obliterated, but they have their place only upon the ground of God's work for all. The promise is for those near and those far, parents and children, free men and slaves.

Further: A fascinating and tremendous disclosure of the Holy One has taken place (comparable only to God's epiphany on Mount Sinai). Fire and storm and shaking of foundations have indicated that it pleased God to make himself felt. Unlike Rudolf Otto, Peter does not speak of an impersonal holy, or mystery; in quoting Psalm 16 he reserves the term "holy" for the Messiah (vs. 27). Perhaps, precisely because he is no historian of religion and no spectator of varieties of religious experiences, he admits that not only he, but everybody, is overwhelmed by the recent manifestation of God. His preaching, then, does not make something relevant; but it shows the incisive and decisive inroad of God and his Spirit upon fleshly men. Only because he relies completely upon God's action, is his preaching powerful.

To continue: The event that has taken place does neither at once overthrow the temple, nor feed hungry mouths, nor reorganize crooked city administrations. Peter's sermon is not prophetic in the sense that it predicts or dictates how the Spirit effects social changes. But it is amazingly full of references to speech. Peter rejoices in announcing a specific mighty act of God: God has given tongues that are understood all over the world. God has given such speech! God is giving understanding! Look, how much the Old Testament explains! Listen to my words! Thus, instead of bothering about the communication problem, Peter explains on what basis it is solved.

Still more is to be said about the occasion: Peter's sermon presupposes that the event to which he points owns a certain ambiguity. All direct witnesses are amazed by it and ask for its meaning (or rather, in Greek, for its essence: "What could this be?" vs. 12). "Others" are ready with an answer: they ascribe the "speech-event" to the influence of alcohol. Judged by psychological, sociological, and moral standards, these critics appear to be irrefutable. What else but disorderly conduct could they see in the disciples' behavior? Read Jer. 23:9, I Cor. 14:23, Eph. 5:18 to realize that biblical authors know of the similarity of phenomena of the Spirit and of intoxicating spirits! Peter preaches in order to dispel the mists of ambiguity.

Finally: like all the sermons recorded in Acts, this sermon does not start out from a biblical text or a given academic topic.

4

Also it does not claim timeless validity. But it is response to an actual event, and as such time-bound, specific, concrete—like the event itself. It does not replace action, but throws light on a present incident. By and in this light, the incident becomes a *historic* event. Without the preacher and his sermon, the mere "facts," such as the babbling tongues, the healing of a lame man (Acts 3-4), the stoning of a radical (7), the appearance of miracle-doing Jews in Hellenistic cities (14), the altar devoted to an unknown god (17), would be mute, ambiguous, delivered to oblivion. But (to change but slightly a statement of Augustine) when the word is added, history is made. Peter's sermon is not only a comment on history or an opinion on its meaning. It makes history.

How can words contribute to the making of history? To answer this question, we turn now away from the background and frame of Peter's sermon, and to its contents. Peter has something to say into the situation in which he stands, he answers questions about it and he lets the power of the witnessed event be radiant. What he says is briefly this:

1. It is not wine ("Who would get drunk at 9 A.M.?") but God—Father, Son, and Spirit—who is present in your midst and causes the amazing things to happen. Both we the speakers and you the hearers are witnesses of nothing less than of God and his work. God acted in memorable fashion not only when he raised Jesus; he does so again, now before your eyes and ears.

2. This means you have no choice whether or not to have anything to do with God. For you are already involved: God has attested Jesus of Nazareth to you with wonders and signs. You had him killed, but God installed him as judge over you. You are murderers—but you will not get away with murder.

The appearance of God in your midst, the shaking of foundations, the language understood by all—this means that the judgment is now.

3. This judgment is amazing: God is not out to avenge himself, but to prove faithful to promises such as Joel's and to be the fulfiller of prayers such as David's. The Jesus whom you killed has been made Lord and Messiah to save what is lost. You could not and did not succeed in removing him. Admit your defeat! Repent! Plea for forgiveness in baptism! Trust the power of the Spirit, all of you!

This is strong and direct preaching. Would that we modern preachers had some of the insight, wisdom, and courage to preach as Peter did! If we possessed it, we would certainly not have to worry about communication. Since we don't, we would at least like to know how Peter came to say what he had to say to those listening to him.

I would like to make the following observations:

1. Peter was "filled with the Holy Spirit" (2:4; 4:8, 31). Obviously, there is no preaching of the prophetic or apostolic sort without the Holy Spirit. It is a gift of God to preach a real sermon. A man has to be born from above, united with the chosen ones of God, looking with unveiled face upon God's glory, moved by the power which comes from God. Some lazy would-be preachers have mistaken this dependence on the Spirit (and the command not to worry, Luke 12:11-12) for a permission not to carefully prepare their sermons. But Peter's sermon shows he has done his homework.

2. Peter makes diligent use of the Bible. We note that he elaborates on no less than three texts (Joel 2:28-32; Ps. 16:8-

6

11; 110:1), but does not treat a single topic given by the Old Testament. His topic, rather, is the day's event, the gift of the Spirit from on high to many fleshly men. The function of the Bible is to give him a key to understand and explain why it is that *God* is proving present and active and manifest, today. The first passage makes him aware that the abundant gift of the Spirit is indicative of the presence of the Lord's day. The second passage shows that the Lord's day and deed are centered on the resurrection of God's chosen one from Hades and corruption. The last Bible text establishes the universal rule of the one enthroned by God. So the Bible instructs Peter, and by referring to the Bible Peter informs others, that Spirit and God's judgment, judgment and the Lord's Messiah, Jesus Christ and Salvation, Salvation and God's triumph over all enemies are inseparable. Had Peter not listened to the Bible, he would have had little or no reason to connect the Spirit with repentance, the resurrection of Jesus with the Messiah's enthronement, the exaltation of the one with salvation for all who call upon his name.

3. But Peter does not only quote and paraphrase the Bible. He also tells of what he, from his own vantage point as an eyewitness, knows of Jesus. He refers to his miracles, his trial and execution, his resurrection and appearance before witnesses. Precisely what Peter has to say about the Messiah Jesus—this is the clutch that holds together the Bible, the present generation, the future salvation of the many; it is the arrow that pierces the heart of the listeners (vs. 37); it is the guarantee that even murderers shall not be eternally lost.

4. The act of preaching is obviously nothing else but putting two and two together. Peter is not an enthusiastic babbler, but to the best of his ability (and of contemporary modes of exegesis), he connects the morning's event with biblical prom-

ise and prayer, and both with Jesus Christ's salvation from death and his saving judgment. We note specifically that he does not start from an analysis of his time and its needs, in order to work his way up to the Scripture and to God—for the present is admittedly ambiguous. Instead, he lets the Bible and Jesus Christ interpret the present.

Two additional remarks may be made. First, Peter does not indicate that the demonstration of God's presence is over with the day of Pentecost. On the contrary, he affirms that the pouring out of the Spirit is to continue (vvs. 17, 38). At a later occasion he asserts (according to Acts 10:47; 11:16) that God is giving the same gift of the Spirit to Gentiles as to Jewish-born disciples.

Second, Peter's preaching does not mean that church and world are nicely set apart. But the very revelation of God which is described is an event occurring for judgment and salvation of both the disciples and those that are still afar. The judgment by the fire-Spirit which begins at God's house is for the salvation of the world.

So much about Peter's sermon.

There are differences between Peter, the Rock, and ministers of twentieth century America. We are not eyewitnesses of Jesus Christ's glory. At best we are but secondary witnesses— until the day of the Parousia (Rev. 1:7). But though our witness to Christ may be infinitely poorer and weaker than that of Peter's, it is still to be a witness to the living and present God. If we dare never point out—driven by the Spirit, enlightened by the Scriptures, centered in the death and resurrection of

8

Christ—that God is acting still in his temple, in the congregation, *and* outside the walls of the holy city, then we have nothing to say and should not pretend that we are preachers. Preaching has nothing to do with an absentee landlord, with a dimming past, with a god who might as well be dead. But it points to the presence of God who is the same yesterday, today, and tomorrow.

THE UNITING WORD

by CONRAD BERGENDOFF

Former President, Augustana College, Rock Island,
Ill.; and former Executive Secretary, Board of
Theological Education, Lutheran Church in
America

ACTS 2:11

When we read the opening verses in the Gospel of St. John
our thoughts go back to the first words of the book of Genesis.
For John, as does the author of Genesis, speaks of the beginning
of the universe. "The Spirit of God," the Old Testament book
says, "was moving over the face of the waters." "In the beginning," the New Testament gospel states, "was the Word."
And when it goes on to say, "the Word was God," we realize
how close is the relationship between God, Word, and Spirit.

There is an Old Testament parallel also to our Pentecostal
lesson about the gift of the Spirit and of the speaking with
tongues. We find it in the story of the building of the tower of
Babel (Gen. 11). There was a time when the "whole earth had
one language." Strangely, the biblical writer adds—"and few
words," which suggests that a happier world could get along
with fewer words. (And are we not warned against a multitude
10

of words in prayer and admonished to speak a more direct "yes" and "no"?)

It was in the development of man's vaulting ambition to build a city which itself would rise to heaven that the Lord intervened. Man was easily tempted to "tall talk," and his vain boasts passed the point where words had reality. In his pride he lost the truth of his words, and soon he was in a state of misunderstanding and disagreement with his fellows. Confusion followed and the building of Babel ceased. The unity of mankind was broken—each went his own way.

This Old Testament parable stands in the background of the events of the first Pentecost. For to Jerusalem had come Jews "from every nation under heaven." The author, Luke, gives a long list of these countries including Parthia, Mesopotamia, Cappadocia, Pontus, Phrygia, Egypt, Libya, Rome, Crete. A glance at the map will show that north, south, east, and west were all represented. These were Jewish residents of the countries named, but they spoke the language of their respective countries and were amazed when they heard each his native language. We are told that the assemblage numbered in the thousands, and the wonderment of the various nationalities was so great because those who were speaking were "all Galileans."

We in our day are no more able than the amazed visitors in Jerusalem on that day to explain how this miracle could take place. But some things in the event are clear, and it is often most helpful in strange circumstances to fasten our attention on what we can understand. And it is abundantly clear that the central light of the story is focused on the proclamation of Jesus Christ. The unusual sound and the mysterious appearance of tongues

11

of flame did not come of themselves, without relationship to a certain time and place. They came as the company of those who had been with Jesus and "were all together in one place." The disciples and others were together in prayer, still trying to understand what had happened these past few months to their Lord and to themselves. Their memories, doubts, hopes, their faith, their fears—all were still mixed up. Only one thing was clear: Christ was risen and therefore all former things had become changed.

Whatever else we may not be able to explain about the happening which to those concerned seemed like a mighty wind and like flames of fire, we can clearly see that it had to do with making known the resurrection of Jesus Christ. No one knew better than Peter what was taking place, and he told the multitude that the Spirit of God was at work. The Jesus whom "you crucified and killed by the hands of lawless men" could not be held in death. "God raised him up," Peter declares time and again, and adds, "of that we are all witnesses."

The speaking of tongues has no meaning apart from the message that is spoken, else it becomes a noise like that of a clanging cymbal. The Spirit that broods over the face of chaos and is present at every new creation brings forth a Word which makes all things new. This Word is Jesus Christ, risen from the dead. "Repent," cries Peter, "and be baptized every one of you in the name of Jesus Christ for the forgiveness of your sins; and you shall receive the gift of the Holy Spirit."

This phenomenon which the crowds were witnessing was not a peculiar possession of the disciples. Through them the Holy

Spirit wanted to descend on every person to enable each one to witness to the risen Christ in whom was forgiveness of sins. "For the promise is to you and to your children and to all that are far off, every one whom the Lord our God calls to him." This manifestation of the presence of the Spirit of God was no strange mystical experience of a coterie of queer characters, but an affirmation of the reconciliation of God and man which makes possible the unification of mankind.

The gift of the Spirit follows the exaltation of Christ; and, one with the Father, he unites all men in his fellowship. "Let all the house of Israel therefore know assuredly that God has made him both Lord and Christ." The selfishness and arrogance of the builders of Babel led to the dispersion of man and the setting up of rival peoples. In the name of Jesus Christ mankind is recalled to its unity under one Lord and Saviour, and the languages of hostile nations are transcended by a Word which is for all peoples and all times.

As in a bud, the whole flower of Christianity is contained in the Pentecostal event. Here is the gift of the Spirit, without which there is no Christian life. Here is the relationship of the Spirit to Christ, who was crucified but who is exalted and who from the throne of the Father grants forgiveness of sins to those who repent. Here, too, is the missionary imperative to make known the gift of the Spirit to men of all nations, and the ecumenical dimension that it is for those near and far that the promise is given. Above all, there is here the uniting Word which can break through all the barriers of cultural and national separation and bring all mankind under the one Lord and God in whom the world has its center and unity. As the light in a prism is gathered and breaks forth into all its component colors, so Pentecost gathers the lines of history before Christ and, by the creative power of the Spirit, spreads forth anew in all directions and all ages.

It is important to notice certain essential qualifications of the ecumenical promise of Pentecost. For example, the promise of the uniting power of the Spirit is tied indissolubly to the person of Jesus Christ. It is in him that the scattered nations find a common Lord. "There is no other name under heaven given among men by which we must be saved." So Peter declared shortly after the day of Pentecost (Acts 4:12). In vain we seek for a common humanity in some anthropological or physical heritage. Nor is education or culture or any political or economic scheme able to unite the minds and hearts of earth's many peoples. Missionaries have used many different kinds of cords brought with them from their homelands to tie close the bonds of old and new churches, but ultimately the only cord that holds is the bond of Jesus Christ. At the heart of its vast humanitarian and organizational structure, the missionary movement has had one real enduring source of power, namely, the gospel: "Repent, and be baptized every one of you in the name of Jesus Christ for the forgiveness of your sins; and you shall receive the gift of the Holy Spirit."

For the Christian church exists for no greater purpose than to proclaim the word of God. This it has received in Holy Scripture, and the cornerstone of Scripture—though time and again rejected by men through the centuries—is Jesus Christ. This Christ, who was crucified, is risen and builds his kingdom in the hearts of men wherever he is acknowledged as the source and ruler of life. He is the all sufficient head under whom the body of mankind finds its unity.

The obverse of this truth is that no other qualifications can become a substitute for the gospel in uniting mankind. We thank God for his church and its life-giving mission through history. But we need to recognize how often churchmen have been tempted to confuse the saving and uniting gospel with human factors. They have deemed their own devices and traditions of equal, and sometimes, seemingly, greater importance than the Word. They have set up a human structure and wanted to confine the Spirit to the house they have built. They have made a traditional form of ministry into an essential element without which the Word could not be considered effective. Indeed, the temptation, even for the churches, has been to build an ecclesiastical tower which would lead directly into heaven and make this alone the entrance. From all of these secondary standards, the result of local developments or one-sided emphases raised to the level of absolutes, the gospel would recall us and would focus our attention on the forgiving power of the Holy Spirit as it is shed abroad in the hearts of those who live by the power of the risen Christ. For "when the goodness and loving kindness of God our Savior appeared, he saved us, not because of deeds done by us in righteousness, but in virtue of his own mercy, by the washing of regeneration and renewal in the Holy Spirit, which he poured out upon us richly through Jesus Christ our Savior, so that we might be justified by his grace and become heirs in hope of eternal life" (Titus 3:4-7). This "saying is sure" even for the ecumenical endeavors of our day.

The unity of God's people is thus a unity around the throne of Christ. It is not primarily an ecclesiastical unity of church structure. To make the organizational unity of all Christians the goal of ecumenicity is to shift the emphasis from the essential to the secondary. A great modern body of Christians under one earthly head would be no more successful or spiritual than was the "corpus christianum" (Christendom) of the medieval centuries. For that proved to be a tower which failed and caused spiritual confusion in all lands. Any movement that emphasizes the body rather than the Head will fail, and no earthly head can take the place of the Christ who rules alone. "My kingdom," He said, "is not of this world." All our worldly trappings will not bring the kingdom, even the good deeds we do in ecclesiastical righteousness. His is a gift of the Spirit, promised to those who receive him in faith, and our churches have meaning only when they proclaim his death and resurrection and the forgiveness of sins whereby we may enter into his fellowship.

Such was the clear proclamation of the disciples on the day of Pentecost, and this is the charter of the church which rightly regards the events of that day as its birth. No less today than in Peter's time it may seem incredible that all of earth's peoples should find their central authority in Jesus Christ. But the disciples were faithful in the proclamation of the risen Lord. They learned the truth of the promise that Christ was for all peoples, and gradually nations near and far off came to his obedience.

We today may feel that it is a hopeless cause to announce Christ as Lord for all of today's nations, races, and religions. Some think to find a common ground for mankind in an evolutionary theory, or in psychological processes, in some economic program or political scheme. Yet these become fragmentary platforms on some level of the tower of Babel. Despite all the human obstacles to unity and deep-rooted divisions of humanity, the church of Christ in the twentieth century has no other message than the gospel of him who was crucified by sinful men but rose from the dead to create a kingdom of forgiven and believing sinners. These Christ would use as the means of uniting mankind around himself, not in some globe-encircling ecclesiastical structure, but in a fellowship of faithful obedience to his will and in a loving relationship to all who call upon his name.

The Spirit that moved on the face of the waters and brought forth a cosmos out of chaos is the same Spirit that breaks through the babel of earth's languages and the walls of humanity's divisions and brings together the scattered parts into a whole. Mankind knows no other name in which such a hope is contained; only the gospel knows of a unity of all creation. The God who created all things uses the church to make known his manifold wisdom and the eternal purpose which he has realized in Christ Jesus our Lord (Eph. 3:9-11). The surrounding multitudes wondered at the sight and sound of the Spirit on the day of Pentecost. We wonder in our day at the movements among the churches which are drawing believers of Christ closer together and teaching them to hear those speaking in what have been foreign tongues. Is it not the same Spirit, working eternally, and saying that to us and our children and our generation is the promise of the unity of the family of God?

THE SUM IS MORE

by EUGENE CARSON BLAKE

Stated Clerk, United Presbyterian
Church in the U. S. A.

"For where two or three are gathered in my name,
there am I in the midst of them."
—MATT. 18:20

Mathematics teaches us that the whole is equal to the sum of
its parts. Experience in other areas of knowledge and life indicates, however, that the sum is often more than the mathematical
addition of parts. We find in chemistry, for example, that we
can add two gases, hydrogen and oxygen, in proper proportions
producing thereby not a mixed gas but liquid water. The sum
here in a very real sense is more than its parts. The sum has
properties that its parts did not have.

I vaguely remember making an experiment once in chemistry
myself in which some chemical substance (the name of which
I have long since forgotten) was used as a catalytic agent. Two
relatively inert substances were put together. Nothing happened.
Then I put in (as directed) the catalytic agent. The two inert
substances soon became a new substance with new and additional properties—the catalyst was itself unchanged. Something
new was added by combination. Social psychologists have long
told us about the surprising behavior of human beings in a

18

crowd. A crowd will often act in ways the individuals separately would not. A mob is something more than the sum of its members.

When I was in college, I played football. In those days eleven men only constituted the first team; the rest were substitutes, used only as a rule when one of the first team was hurt or weary. There were two men on our team who added more to it when they were playing than their own individual skills. With them in the game, as they usually were, we were a team. Without them we were eleven men trying to play together. You couldn't put your finger on exactly what it was that they brought with them but when both of them were hurt in the last quarter of the last game I ever played, their loss was too much for us to stand. Yale won in the last six minutes—one of the major tragedies of my life up to that point.

There is an old story told of a man who was discussing religion with a minister in front of the open coal fire in the living room of the manse. The man was arguing that there was no need for him to be a part of the church, that he could be as good a Christian, maybe better, as an individual committed to God. While he was talking the minister did not interrupt but, picking up the poker, steered one red hot coal from the others and let it lie alone on the hearth. He didn't have to speak to answer. His point was demonstrably clear when the lone coal quickly lost its fire and turned ashen gray.

It is about this vital relationship of the church to individual Christian faith and living that I speak. The point is this: When individuals are associated in a church, there is more there than the sum of the individuals. Jesus gave his first disciples this promise: "Where two or three are gathered in my name, there am I in the midst of them." It is the presence of Jesus in the midst which changes a group of Christians into a church. Yes, it is his promise that he is here now that makes our gathering far more significant than the sum of us as individuals.

I.

What is the church? To answer that question it is well to state first what the church is not. The church is not a building. A church building is important but it is always secondary. It is a tool. Children and some older people think of some building when they hear the word church, but a church is not its building.

Again, the church is not an organization. In these days the church is rather highly organized. There are committees everywhere. Responsibility for various jobs is parceled out. There are many reports and much mimeographing. Now important as all this may be, a church is not its organization. Organization is secondary. Organization is a tool. Organization is to serve the church.

Again, the church is not a program. Some people try to define a church by telling what is done by it. They say that the church is its worship, its teaching, and its service. A church, to be a church, must perform these vital acts but the activities, the program, are not the church. It is all important, but program is secondary. It is either a tool or a product. Even the program is not the church.

The church, furthermore, is something more and other than the denomination. Our denomination is an important part of the religious and community life of the nation, but it is not the church. The denomination is secondary. It is a tool but it is not the church.

What, then, is the church? Well, the church is people. The church is essentially a gathering of people. The Christian church is the gathering of people in the name of Christ. A word, however, needs to be said in explanation of this Hebraic biblical expression: the name of Christ. Whenever in the Bible you see the word, name, it always means something more than a personal label. To the Hebrews a name was not merely your identification but also an index of your character and spirit. Name meant more, even, than reputation as we sometimes use it. The name is the person.

This gathering, then, of people (which is the Christian church) in the name of Christ is a group or fellowship of people bound together in his spirit. Any group of people in more or less intimate relationship in the spirit of Jesus Christ is at least a part of the Christian church.

This is the reason, despite all the unhappy and sinful divisions of the church in belief, program, worship, organization, and denomination, the church is yet essentially one. And Christians who are part of the church recognize one another across all walls and boundaries of difference. For the true spirit of Jesus is inclusive, appreciative; moral, yes, but it does not judge; has convictions, yes, but is not divisive.

The church, then, is people added together—but something more, some one more, is added. Jesus himself is spiritually present according to his promise. "Where two or three are gathered together in my name, there am I in the midst of them."

This is essentially what happened at Pentecost. The account runs: "When the day of Pentecost was fully come, they (the disciples) were all with one accord in one place." There were the conditions. Jesus awaited that moment—a gathering of his disciples in one accord in one place. Then and only then came Jesus in the power of the Spirit. Let us remember, then, in all our decisions about the church, its buildings, its organization, its program, and its interrelationships, that the church is basically people gathered in accord in the spirit of Jesus Christ. This is fundamental. Here is the power.

II.

Granted such a definition of what the church is, we need, then, to raise the second question: How important is it?

Here we find ourselves torn between two extremes and conflicting answers. The non-Christian world grants the church a place among its other institutions, along with government, schools, fraternities, and clubs; in our time attaching less and less importance to it relative to labor unions, manufacturers associations, and communities of scholars.

On the other hand, Christians have generally been so much impressed with the divine importance of the church that they have been unable to see its wrongs or weaknesses. I hope that the definition I have given of the church as a gathering of people in the name of Christ may help us better to assess its importance. As long as we remember that the church consists of people we won't be too much surprised at its sins and weaknesses. But if we believe that Christ himself is the heart of it, that it is his body, his bride, then we shall see its significance and begin to understand why it has lasted and how it has made our world what it is. The Christian church is the most important fellowship of people in the whole world for two reasons.

1. It is, in the first place, the creative basis of our culture, civilization, and government. Remember I am not speaking about the buildings, programs, or organization of the church. I speak of the consensus of people, the integrated fellowship of the disciples of Jesus Christ, and him in their midst. Our greatest pictures, our greatest music, our greatest drama, our

greatest literature have stemmed from Jesus Christ and the gathering of his people which is the church—even governments. I do not mean to say that the governments of the Western world are to be confused with the righteousness of the Kingdom of God—far from it. But I say to you with all seriousness that the honesty, altruism, and respect for human personality, the self-sacrifice and sense of human community that orderly and decent government and civilization require, have been, so far as we have had them, the gift of the Christian church to the Western world. For what breaks down government when it collapses? You and I know that it is moral collapse: divisive bloc mentality, hatreds of class, envy, stealing, killing, race prejudice, and irreconcilable factionalism. These are what destroy civilization, culture, and government.

Today, due to the shrinking of our world, the basic problems of order and civilization are world-wide and not national or community. Some naively hope by establishing committees to establish a stable world government. Though I fully share the purpose and ends of those who urge the giving up of some sovereignty by the nations as the ultimate hope of peace, I suggest to you that what the Christian church is doing and has been doing to throw bridges across the gulfs that separate us from one another is much more to the point than setting up blueprints of how a world government might work. The missionaries you have been sending, the relief to which you have contributed, the refugee families you have received—these are the kind of things that are the foundation of the one world we all desire if you do these things truly in the name of Christ.

2. There is a second reason why I believe that the church, as I have defined it, is the most important fellowship of people in the world. The church is our only alternative to, and effective force against, godless collectivism. Irreligious Americans

have been feverishly looking for some effective alternative to communism. There is only one good alternative—the Christian church. (Again let me remind you I speak not of organization, program, building, or sect.) I say there is only one good alternative to communism. There are other alternatives. Hitler offered one. Mussolini another. Moscow and Peking are patterns seriously offered. Fascism, ecclesiastic or political, would have you believe that it is the only alternative to Marxism and Russian communism. They forget or discount the Christian church. The true alternative we face is between godless collectivism on the one hand and free and responsible civilization on the other; a civilization grows wherever the Christian church is a powerful influence.

If our rich men think that they can beat communism and socialism by becoming fascists they will get the revolution they deserve. The tension of our times, which shows itself in all sorts of ways these days—in a school tax election, in politics with wild charges and countercharges being made—can lead to nothing but chaos and totalitarian collectivism in the end unless—unless there is a Christian church which draws men together in faith in Christ and humble adherence to Christ's standards which can serve as the basis for the new kind of techniques and government that the modern world demands. There is no going back. We go forward; willy-nilly, we go forward. The Christian church offers the only alternative to godless collectivism on the right or left.

Primitive man worked hard and found his place in society because he hardly knew himself as an individual. He was part of the clan and hardly distinguished himself from it. As civilization progressed, men became more and more conscious of their separate importance as individuals. But as the world has now grown more crowded, the re-establishment of more intimate relations than earlier days required is now obviously needed. Once it made no difference to us what happened in Europe or Asia. Now these nations are at our door. The fellowship that is in Jesus Christ is the hope of one world and the only hope if men would be free and responsible. Such is the importance of the church when guided and sustained by God's Holy Spirit.

A VIOLENT BLAST OF WIND

by KEITH R. BRIDSTON

Professor of Systematic Theology, Pacific
Lutheran Theological Seminary, Berkeley, Calif.

Pentecost is romantic. So is the ecumenical movement. That is its greatest danger. For the strange and wonderful and "exotic" fascination of the work of the Holy Spirit may distract us from the earth-bound realities of churchly existence. The Holy Spirit does indeed work in spectacular ways. We are, as those on the first Pentecost, "perfectly amazed," when we are confronted by the extraordinary power of God at work among men in a dramatic way.

But the Holy Spirit does not always work in such overt fashion. Nor does he work in a way that we can always so easily recognize. To discern these "quiet" and paradoxical movements of the Spirit is one of the most difficult, *and* most crucial, tasks in ecumenical participation.

It is, therefore, essential in trying to understand the ecumenical significance of Pentecost for today to see the work of the Holy Spirit throughout the *whole* story of the early church as it is presented to us in the Acts of the Apostles. For the "tongues of flame" and the "violent blast of wind" (Goodspeed translation) are marks of the church found all through church history. The "flame" and the "wind," however, are often hidden and quiet; and their "violent" character is not appreciated unless the ear is quick and the eye keen—that is, unless it is apprehended by the eye and ear of faith.

For example, Pentecost must be compared with the Jerusalem council, recorded later in Acts, to understand the fullness of the Spirit's ecumenical work in the church. For it is in both events that the full dimensions of the Holy Spirit's sanctifying energy are evidenced. What are the distinguishing features of that "violent" Spirit as he "calls, gathers, and enlightens" the ecumenical assembly then and now?

In the first place, an ecumenical assembly is occasioned by *confusion.* In the case of the Jerusalem meeting the cause of the confusion was the problem of the integration of Jewish and Gentile converts in the church. This was, indeed, a problem of Christian unity: how was the unity of the Christian community to be maintained in the face of the growing ethnic complexity of the body? The apostles were accused of "turning the world upside down" by the civil authorities; in the process they were also upsetting the church. In short, the expansion of the church was threatening its original unity, and confusion resulted; it was therefore imperative that the leaders of the church should assemble to consider these matters.

In the same way, we are also faced with ecumenical confusion. We are becoming increasingly aware that the separation of the Christian body into separated confessional and denominational bodies is not only abnormal, but indeed a denial of the essential character of the church. In a new and immediate way, Paul's scandalized query: "Is Christ divided?" is being brought home to us. If the ecumenical movement can be called "the great new fact," part of its newness rests in the fact that our eyes are being opened to the state of ecumenical confusion in which we find ourselves. And faced with this confusion we also are being led by the Holy Spirit to assemble for consideration of these matters.

In the second place, *conference* is an authentic mark of the ecumenical community. Faced with their difficulties, the apostles conferred; they met together in conference. They could not solve the problem of Christian unity which they faced in mutual isolation, and so they assembled. As John Wesley once said: "The Bible knows nothing of a solitary Christian." One of the geniuses of the ecumenical movement has been its recovery of this primitive Christian tradition: to meet in conference.

Of course, in the present day we feel almost overwhelmed by the number of meetings which church life seems to involve. But let that not overshadow the spiritual and theological significance of true ecumenical assembly. When, therefore, in the constitution of the Commission of Faith and Order it states: "Its main work is to draw churches out of isolationism into conferences, in which none is to be asked to be disloyal to or to compromise its convictions, but to seek to explain them to others while seeking to understand their points of view," one should recognize a line of ecumenical tradition which reaches back not just to 1910 or 1920 or 1927, but to that ecumenical assembly in Jerusalem recorded for us in the Acts of the Apostles.

In the third place, *contention* is an indispensable attribute of ecumenical assemblies. It is sometimes assumed that ecumenical participation means compromise—the playing up of our points of agreement and a covering up of our points of difference: in short, that "ecumenical" denotes a movement of toleration. But, as Karl Barth wrote in a preparatory paper for the Faith and Order World Conference in 1937: "The concept of toleration originates in political and philosophical principles which are not only alien but even opposed to the Gospel." In other words, authentic ecumenical movement never sacrifices truth to advance unity.

Needless to say, our different *conceptions* of truth are not to be equated with *the* Truth, which is Jesus Christ; but even our different conceptions of truth cannot be simply ignored or glossed over insofar as they have anything to do with *the* Truth at all. And it is for this reason that ecumenical assembly is marked by live contention rather than passive toleration, engagement with one another rather than casual acceptance.

The Faith and Order constitution (which, by the way, embodies many of the fundamental principles of ecumenical participation) exemplifies this by guaranteeing that "irreconcilable differences are to be recorded as honestly as agreements," in all its theological discussions and conferences. This has been accepted by the World Council of Churches as its guiding principle as well. Here again, this is an ecumenical tradition which does not just date back fifty years or so but one which can be traced all the way through to the apostles who, as the writer of Acts makes clear, debated, contended, argued—because they were concerned to maintain their unity *in truth*.

Read the fifteenth chapter of Acts again, carefully, and without your stained-glass spectacles, to see the tensions and controversies which arose out of the assembly of the saints! So it must be today when many of the great verities of the Christian faith are at stake in our meetings. Without Christian controversy— that speaking the truth in love—the ecumenical movement would soon degenerate and die.

Even in the advance of secular knowledge this principle is authenticated; as Alfred North Whitehead writes: "In formal logic, a contradiction is the signal of a defeat; but in the evolution of real knowledge it marks the first step in progress towards a victory."[1] We contend, then, not *against* one another, but *with* one another for the truth.

Perhaps in this perspective we see something new in the great theological controversies of Christian history. As G. K. Chesterton puts it: "It is exactly this which explains what is so inexplicable to all the modern critics of the history of Christianity. I mean the monstrous wars about small points of theology, the earthquakes of emotion about a gesture or a word. It was only a matter of an inch; but an inch is everything when you are balancing. . . . Remember that the Church went in specifically for dangerous ideas; she was a lion tamer."[2]

In the past these controversies often culminated in division; in the ecumenical movement it is our hope that our controversies will issue in unity. In that sense, we are seeing in our time a great reversal of Christian history from the movement of "reformation-separation" to "reformation-reconciliation."

In the fourth place, ecumenical assembly leads to *conclusions*. Ecumenical meetings may attract their share of those who are just "Ecclesiastical Globe-Trotters," as one dubbed them, coming along for the ride. But real ecumenical assemblies come together for a purpose. As William Temple, Chairman of the Faith and Order Movement, said at the Edinburgh Conference in 1937: "Divisions cannot be healed by the reiterated statement of them. . . . Our churches have sent us here to confer about our differences with a view to overcoming them." However slow and painful the progress may be, each ecumenical assembly has come to certain conclusions which are testimonies to the fact that they are a part of an ecumenical *movement*.

[1] *Science and the Modern World* (New York: Macmillan Co., 1925) ; paperback, Mentor Books, 1948, p. 186.
[2] *Orthodoxy* (London: John Lane & Co., 1908), p. 184.

At that first Jerusalem assembly, the Christians also came to conclusions after their debates and deliberations: "Then pleased it the apostles and elders, with the whole church, to send chosen men of their own company to Antioch with Paul and Barnabas . . . And they wrote letters by them after this manner. . . . It seemed good unto us, being assembled with one accord, to send chosen men unto you with our beloved Barnabas and Paul . . . So when they were dismissed, they came to Antioch: and when they had gathered the multitude together, they delivered the epistle."

In other words, the Jerusalem council resulted in an agreement which was conveyed to the churches, "which when they had read, they rejoiced for the consolation." Is this not in essence what a modern ecumenical assembly seeks also—a conference resulting in conclusions which bring consolation to the churches?

Finally, in the fifth place, ecumenical assembly eventually leads to *conflagration*. The epistle from the Jerusalem council not only confirmed the gospel already preached among the established churches; even more importantly, it led to a continuation and extension of the missionary labors of the apostles and a revival of evangelistic endeavor in the congregations: "And as they went through the cities, they delivered the decrees for to keep, that were ordained of the apostles and elders which were at Jerusalem. And so were the churches established in the faith, and increased in number daily."

And this is also the goal of the ecumenical movement today: both to strengthen the ties of unity between the churches spread throughout the world and to stimulate them to carry the gospel to the uttermost parts of the earth and to all men.

Bishop Lesslie Newbigin has given us a sober warning of a "false sort of ecumenism" . . . the search for wider Christendom "without the hard demands of missionary obedience." As he says: "The ecumenical movement has been a by-product of the missionary movement . . . The ecumenical movement will become fatally corrupted if it does not remain true to its missionary origins."[3]

The theme of "Mission and Unity" which we might identify with only the present-day ecumenical movement is, therefore, the most ancient ecumenical tradition of all. Every ecumenical assembly worthy of that name is, by definition, concerned with the indivisible relationship between the unity of the church and the mission of the church. It has been so since the apostles and elders and brethren met in Jerusalem those many centuries ago.

The delegates to the Third World Conference on Faith and Order at Lund, Sweden, in 1952 affirmed:

"The measure of unity which it has been to the Churches to experience together must now find clearer manifestation. A faith in the One Church of Christ which is not implemented by *acts* of obedience is dead. There are truths about the nature of God and His Church which will remain forever closed to us unless we act together in obedience to the unity which is already ours."

It is in such ringing assertions of ecumenical faith that our common concern for the unity and mission of the church is raised up in a confession echoing through the world and in continuity with the Christian community throughout the ages. Vision leads to action and action results in vision. Let us pray that God will open our eyes and lead us on the way in our ecumenical pilgrimage.

[3] *Household of God* (New York: Friendship Press, 1954), p. 10.

THE THRILL OF BEING CHOSEN

by EDGAR M. CARLSON

President, Gustavus Adolphus College,
St. Peter, Minn.

JOHN 15:16, 17

Let us understand our objective from the outset! I hope to persuade you that the great thrill and excitement of life is not so much the privilege of choosing as the high honor of being chosen.

In terms of the specifically Christian implications of this fact, I propose to assert that personal faith and life acquire stability and dynamic out of the sure knowledge that Christ has chosen us, instead of our choosing him. Christ is not one of our choices; we are among those whom he has chosen. Moreover, it is this common knowledge on the part of the Christian community which really unites all who confess the name of Christ and seek to do his will. The basis for the unity of the church does not lie in agreement among its members with respect to their choices, but rather in a common confession and witness that Christ has chosen them.

We have it on Jesus' authority, do we not? "You did not choose me, but I chose you and appointed you that you should go and bear fruit and that your fruit should abide; so that whatever you ask the Father in my name, he may give it to you.

This I command you, to love one another." Let us listen to what this Word of our Lord may have to say to his scattered and divided brethren in this sixth decade of the twentieth century.

Of course, the freedom to choose is one of the great and inalienable rights. It is one of our most treasured freedoms. Any restrictions on it run counter to the spirit of democracy and of our time, even when the choices at issue seem to be relatively unimportant. What is at issue is something which affects human dignity; we claim freedom to choose as a right. The right is limited only by the right of others also to choose freely.

This is a real limitation and it is governed by laws which establish directions and guidelines for actions which do not collide with the freedom of choice of others. Or, more accurately, the laws represent a consensus as to what governing regulations will yield the largest measure of freedom to the largest number of people and will safeguard the essential freedoms of all. In a measure, then, our freedom constitutes a privilege which is granted by the community, state, or nation.

But it is equally clear that we can restrict our own freedom by the choices which we make. Unless we choose wisely, our subsequent choices will be reduced. The young man or woman who chooses not to continue his education has narrowed the range of choices which will be open in the future. If we act consistently on the safest and least challenging alternative, we will discover that our live options become increasingly fewer and less demanding.

In a significant measure, life is made up of what has been chosen. The priorities which a student gives to the various options open to him, with respect to his time and energies and devotion, largely determine the kind of person he will be. The priorities which parents give in the things they choose may determine not only the kind of persons they will be but also to some extent the kind of persons their children will become.

So, the choices we make are exceedingly important. But the thrill and excitement of making a choice cannot really hold a candle to the thrill and excitement of being chosen. The astonished gasp of surprise and delight which the photographer tries so hard to catch when the winner is announced in almost any kind of contest is genuine. The candidate for public office who wins the endorsement of his party convention, or the endorsement of the voters at the polls, provides adequate pictorial evidence that there is a great thrill in being chosen.

At any level, it is a great satisfaction to know that one enjoys the confidence of his fellows. To get the job you wanted, or the promotion—there is genuine satisfaction in that. And what compares with that deep and solemn joy of being chosen in love by the one who has taken your heart captive? Here it is not enough that one shall be free to choose. To choose and not be chosen—this is deepest anguish. There is a time when one wants to be free to choose whom he will, but permanent and satisfying attachments require that one shall have moved beyond this. Then everything depends upon being chosen by the loved one.

Jesus said to his disciples, "You did not choose me, but I chose you . . . " I suppose they could have argued with him about that if they had been disposed. They could have talked about how they had made decisions which put them into his company and made them a part of that itinerant band of followers. But they did not argue the point. There was something solemn and awesome and holy about having been chosen by him in whom they had come to believe.

It is an evidence of shallowness and immaturity in our

religious commitment that we are so prone to consider it one of the electives in life. People choose whether or not to be religious, and then which religion they prefer, and which church they shall join. How wrong we are!

Who decided that God should be there in the heavens bringing a world into being and peopling it with multitudes and generations, one of whom should bear your name? You did not decide that he should be the creator and you the creature, or that he whose glory is above the heavens should come to be a living presence in the Babe of Bethlehem. You did not decide that the Bible, his Word, should be written and transmitted through the generations of believers; or that there should come into being a church which is his living body through which he would reach out to lay his hand on you and give you an assignment.

That we have come to stand in the company of those who believe, or even of those who listen, is his choice more than yours. There may or may not be the inner turmoil and excitement that generally attends being chosen by a loved one to share his or her life, but there is no lasting satisfaction and solid joy like that which comes from the knowledge that we have been chosen by God through Jesus Christ, that we have been commissioned by him to an assignment that engrosses and engages all of time and eternity besides.

Moreover, it must be asserted without reservation that this statement of our Lord applies to everyone who hears it. It is not only for those who have "left all to follow him," not only for the religiously committed or those who profess to be Christians. No one is left out; no one is excused. You have been chosen! You have been elected! You have a royal commission—do not treat it as though it were something spoken in jest, or idle chatter with which we regale ourselves to pass the time away.

"I chose you . . . " He who speaks these words is that strong Son of Man in whom dwelt all the fullness of God, who because he was raised from the dead and exalted to God's right hand is the contemporary of every man and every age. He is the eternal Word, the Logos of God, which was in the beginning, without which nothing was made that has been made, and who shall be there at the end to judge the living and the dead.

"I have chosen you . . . " This means that every man's life has a purpose. We need not narrowly conceive of that purpose, as though there was only one thing that we could do with the sanction and blessing of God. Indeed, Jesus says, "I have chosen you and appointed you that you should go and bear fruit and that your fruit should abide." Whether he has appointed us to be ministers or doctors or technicians, and whether in one place or another, is incidental to the major appointment which is that we shall bear fruit and that our fruit should abide.

There is no more nagging doubt to be encountered in life than the question whether what one is doing is part of what really needs to be done, and whether it will matter in the end. There is no more terrible fate than to come to the end of one's life, without any chance to do it over again ever, and have to feel that all of his life he has been chasing will-o'-the-wisps, doing things that didn't really need to be done and failing ever to come to grips with the substance of life itself. We need to set our lives and our tasks within the perspective of his kingdom, so that we do things for the right reasons and from the right motives, if our daily routine is to be lifted up into a commission from the Lord. Then, even the cup of water, given in his name, registers as part of a great commission.

What I have been saying is that this conviction that we have been chosen by God is the proper fulcrum for our faith. It gives us the leverage we need against the nagging doubts and the haunting skepticism, and against the solvents of ethical relativism and subjectivism which tend to dissolve the content and structure of faith so that it merges indistinguishably with the general landscape. We can never be sure, as long as the focus is upon our own choice, whether it has been genuinely made, or whether it has been made from the right motives. But if he has chosen us, this is a different matter.

If, in addition, he has chosen everyone else, we are saved from the assumption that we have been chosen at the expense of others or in preference to others. Indeed, we have been chosen to bear fruit, and the particular fruit which is appropriate to the choice is "to love one another." This is the commandment. The choice and the commandment apply to all men. The Christian is distinguished from others only in that he acknowledges that this is the case. He has been chosen by God, through Christ, for the purpose of loving others.

What has just been said needed to be said, because the conviction that we have been chosen can lead to exclusiveness. If it is ever assumed that our election is to privilege without responsibility, we may easily become archenemies of the kingdom. History provides adequate illustrations of "messianic complexes" that have been far removed from the "calling and election" which issues in the fruit of love.

But the assumption that religion is a private matter, one of our options, something that we choose, also plays havoc with the gospel of our Lord. It destroys the genuine sense of unity in the Body of Christ and makes of the Christian faith little more than a consensus among people in matters of spiritual interest. One man's religious ideas are as valid as another's and the religious fellowship comes to be a fellowship among reasonably like-minded people. Theoretically, the various denominations are considered to reflect different consensuses about the Christian faith, represented in different patterns of beliefs.

Historically, divisions have come into being in part because of such doctrinal disagreements, though it is almost a truism today that the range of theological diversity which exists within any given denomination is much greater than that which exists between some median viewpoint within each of the denominations. But whatever the explanation or justification for the fragmented state of the Christian church may be is of secondary importance to the main question which is whether the church is something over which we preside—which we have chosen—or something over which Christ presides because he has chosen it.

The answer to this question is clear. When Jesus addressed the twelve disciples, he was not merely addressing twelve individuals. He was addressing those to whom he was entrusting the gospel and whom he was charging with the great commission to bring it to all the nations even to the end of time. He was describing their mission when he would no longer be present with them in the flesh—when his Spirit would be guiding and directing them from within. Pentecost would come and it would verify what he had been saying. There would come to them the overwhelming sense of having been chosen to bear his gospel to the world. The confused and frightened band, remembering their failures and unable to forget their hopes, would be transformed into the fearless champions of the crucified and risen Christ, King of Kings, Lord of Lords. We are part of the church that was represented by the disciples and which has inherited their apostleship. We have been chosen to bear fruit which may abide. The inevitable and inescapable commandment is that we "love one another."

There is one other rubric in this text. It still needs to be there. We have been chosen "so that whatever you ask the Father in my name, he may give it to you." As individuals and as churches we need to be reminded of that. One of the implications of being chosen is that we are invited to pray, with the full endorsement of Christ and in the conviction that the Father will give us what we need. It's a great privilege to have that open access to the throne of God. To be petitioners together before that throne brings us, as individuals and churches, together.

There is a prayer of Ignatius Loyola which, it seems to me, might well bring our thought to a conclusion and illustrate our point besides:

Teach me, Good Lord, to serve Thee as Thou deservest; to give and not to count the cost, to fight and not to heed the wounds; to toil and not to seek for rest; to labor and not to ask for any reward, save that of knowing that I do Thy will, through Jesus Christ, the Lord. Amen.

TOGETHER IN ONE PLACE

by WILLIAM B. CATE

Executive Secretary, Greater Portland
Council of Churches

"When the day of Pentecost had come, they were
all together in one place. . . And they were all
filled with the Holy Spirit. . ."

—ACTS 2:1, 4

Recently a denomination in the separatist tradition held a
national convention in our city. In a major address to the
assemblage, one of the leaders of the communion was reported
to have said that the ecumenical movement, as now constituted,
was stifling the spiritual vitality of the churches involved. He
was of the opinion that the numerous mergers occurring among
denominations had resulted not in strengthening them but in
weakening them. It was his conviction that the ecumenical
movement as we know it was not of the Holy Spirit. The resulting conclusion we inevitably must draw from his statements
is that, for him, disunity and division are more important contemporary sources of spiritual renewal than the current great
ground swell for Christian unity.

A study of our text describing the Christians gathered at
Pentecost seems to tell another story. It tells of Christians being
together: "When the day of Pentecost had come, they were all

41

together in one place . . . And they were all filled with the Holy Spirit. . . ." In the mind of the writer, Luke, there appears to be a direct relationship between the fact that all the early disciples were gathered in one place at Pentecost and the fact that the Holy Spirit descended upon them in its fullness. Let us look more closely at the ramifications of this scripture for unity today.

On the Jewish Feast of Pentecost, the frightened and uncertain band of Christian disciples gathered in Jerusalem. Their continuing loyalty to Christ brought them to this place. Undoubtedly they congregated with the words of Jesus in mind, "For where two or three are gathered in my name, there am I in the midst of them" (Matt. 18:20).

People meet for countless reasons. It may be for sociability, business, political or religious purposes. Criminals band together to plan their crimes. Communists huddle in their cell groups to draft strategies for world revolution. Armies mass in one place for battle. But Christians meet in the name of Christ to worship him and to talk about what he has done. It was important that on the day of Pentecost the disciples were not meeting simply for a social purpose but rather to honor Christ.

Obedience to Christ has always been the trumpet call to unity in the Christian church. A survey of ecumenical literature and the records of ecumenical conferences discovers many references to Ephesians 2:14: "For he is our peace, who has made us both one, and has broken down the dividing wall of hostility." The prayer of Jesus in John 17:20, 21 has undoubtedly been the most widely used scripture as the basis of our unity: ". . . that they all may be one . . . so that the world may believe that thou hast sent me." When the world and national ecumenical bodies were organized, the doctrinal preambles stating the basis of unity were always centered in Jesus Christ as

Lord. The preamble of the World Council of Churches confesses, "Jesus Christ as God and Savior." The churches that unite in the National Council of Churches declare Jesus Christ as "divine Lord and Savior."

The Christian church exists because of what God has done for all men in Jesus Christ. The unity that we seek is but a oneness that God has revealed in Christ. The writer of Ephesians states it clearly, "And he came and preached peace to you who were far off and peace to those who were near; for through him we both have access in one Spirit to the Father" (Ephesians 2:17). Our loyalty to Christ unites us. At the third World Faith and Order Conference held at Lund, Sweden, in 1952 the delegates were able to say: "As we seek to draw closer to Christ we come closer to one another."[1] On the first Christian Pentecost, as today, his followers came together in his name to worship him.

The second ecumenical insight from the text is that "they were all together in one place." It was important that they were all together. However, Luke seems to be stressing the point that not only were they together but *all* were there *in one place.* Apparently their total presence in the one locality in a spirit of harmony and common concern contributed in a significant way to the descent of the Holy Spirit.

An experience of joy has come to many Christian people from diverse separated traditions in our community as we have participated in theological conversations involving the doctrinal issues that separate us. The joy which is of the Holy Spirit comes when we begin to emerge out of our isolation and alienation from one another into contact and communication. Stereotypes, fears, and anxieties are dispelled, and a new freedom of

[1] Oliver S. Tompkins (ed.), *The Third World Conference on Faith and Order,* Lund, 1952 (London: SCM Press, 1953), p. 5.

the spirit comes when we meet face to face and humbly discuss our common faith. God's renewing love enters to cleanse human relations polluted by fear and suspicion when people become open to one another and to God. The author of I John 4:18 writes, "There is no fear in love, but perfect love casts out fear."

About a month after arriving at my present position, I was visited by two Roman Catholic priests and a Roman Catholic layman, the latter being the executive of the local office of the National Conference of Christians and Jews. They asked me to participate in a church-state symposium to be held on the campus of a Roman Catholic university. The symposium was to deal with delicate church-state issues that have long been points of tension among Roman Catholics and Protestants. I had come to Oregon from one of the most conservative and unco-operative Roman Catholic dioceses in the United States. As a result, my immediate reaction was that of one about to be taken advantage of and "used." Fortunately, trust won out over fear and I became involved in an annual interfaith experience that has added greatly to the good will of our region.

But of more importance to me, personally, was the sense of release from my anxieties once I realized that these people were sincere in their overtures of good will. They helped to free me from the chains of my own misconceptions and fears. In communion between Christians, God's Holy Spirit enters in, breaking down the walls of hostility that separate us. By love through Christ we are reconciled one to another, "For he is our peace who has made us both one." Reuel Howe speaks powerfully to our situation: "The power of love is liberating. . . . The great Christian word is redemption, which means transforming a destructive relationship into one in which the conditions and purposes of love are realized."[2]

[2] Reuel L. Howe, *Herein Is Love* (Valley Forge: Judson Press, 1961), p. 58.

They were not *only* all together. The disciples were also in *one* place. This phrase, "in one place," slightly modified, has been incorporated into one of the finest statements ever written on the nature of the unity we seek. It is the statement on unity of the Third Assembly of the World Council of Churches held at New Delhi, India, in 1961. The statement substitutes the word "each" for the word "one." It says: "We believe that the unity which is both God's will and his gift to his church is being made visible as *all in each place* who were baptized into Jesus Christ and confess him as Lord and Savior are brought by the Holy Spirit into one fully committed fellowship."[3]

This statement seems to indicate that the ecumenical movement as manifest in the world, national, state, and local councils of churches will only become real as it takes on more vitality in and among the congregations in a community. At present, the ecumenical movement appears to prosper more the farther it is from the life of the local congregation. Yet, when the spirit came at Pentecost they were all together in one place. The ecumenical scandal today is on Main Street where Christian fellowship is maintained on an area denominational basis and a congregation rarely has significant association with neighboring congregations across the street. In the light of the Pentecost scripture, how can the Holy Spirit enter into the church life of the average American community in its fullness when so much estrangement among Christians still exists?

Christians are made to be together. We are all a part of one body, says St. Paul. One part of the body cannot thrive by itself. If all the body were a single organ where would the body be? The church is composed of diverse functions, but each part is needed and cannot say to another part we have no need of you.

---

[3] W. A. Visser 't Hooft (ed.), *The New Delhi Report* (New York: Association Press, 1962), p. 116.

The third insight of our text is that after they were all together in one place, "They were filled with the Holy Spirit." After the Pentecostal experience, a great expression of love flowed into the life of the Christian church. The greatest gift of the Holy Spirit is love. Luke writes, "And all who believed were together and had all things in common. . . And day by day, attending the temple together and breaking bread in their homes, they partook of food with glad and generous hearts, praising God and having favor with all people" (Acts 2:44, 46-47). The fellowship of Christians assembled at Pentecost became one people when the one spirit flowed into their lives. The first inclination was to pool their resources and to do all things together.

The effect of the Holy Spirit in the lives of Christians is to make them more loving. The mood of Pentecost is reflected in I John 4:7, "Beloved, let us love one another; for love is of God, and he who loves is born of God and knows God." Thus, Luke concludes the second chapter of Acts with the report that the community of love of the early Christians found favor with all people and grew rapidly. The fact that Christians were together as one people and manifested a high level of love for one another and the people of the world, would seem to be the principal reason for their numerical success.

Love comes after the Holy Spirit. The twelfth chapter of First Corinthians which deals with the Spirit and the "one body" is followed by the thirteenth chapter which is St. Paul's great hymn of love. It has been my experience in co-operative Christian action in the local community that when Christians gather in Christ's name and seek to be obedient to him, God's Holy Spirit does enter into their midst. Motivation develops to express their love in service to their fellowmen in the world. Roman Catholics and Protestants in our city, after two years of

46

dialogue on a theological level, became restive and made plans to become jointly involved in concerns of racial justice and world peace. Unity and the mission of the Church are completely interrelated.

May the prayer of our Lord that they all may be one become our prayer as well. May it be our prayer, also, that all of Christ's people in every community will gather together as one people to manifest Christ's love to the world and thereby receive the gift of the Holy Spirit in its fullness. The experience of the early Christians on Pentecost can also be the experience of the church today.

BEGINNING AT PENTECOST

by SAMUEL McCREA CAVERT

Former General Secretary, National Council of
the Churches of Christ in the U.S.A.

"I speak concerning Christ and the Church."
—EPHESIANS 5:32

What happened at Pentecost? You may get confused answers
to the question, even from those who faithfully commemorate
the event. The symbolic pictures of the activity of the Holy
Spirit—the rushing wind, the flaming fire, the strange
tongues—are too full of mystery to be comprehended clearly.
But one fact of history is beyond question: the *result* of Pentecost was the emergence of the new community that we call the
Christian church. From that day to this there has been a continuous fellowship of the Spirit, centered in Christ and em-
bodied in the church.

Pentecost is therefore a time for thinking about the church,
and especially about the church as seen in its formative stage
and as related to the churches of today.

Nowhere in the Bible do we find a formal definition of the
church. There is, instead, a great wealth of figures of speech
and poetic images which suggest—more vividly than any literal
description—how we are to understand it. A careful scholar
has listed more than eighty distinctive ways in which the Chris-

tian community is pictured in the New Testament.[1] We shall consider two of them. It is a chastening but salutary experience to discover how different are these biblical views of the church from the way in which the average churchman thinks of his church today.

I

One of the basic understandings of the church in the Bible is that it is *The People of God*. This interpretation carries us behind the New Testament into our heritage from the Old. Indeed, it is the theme of a People of God, called to carry out his purpose for mankind, which is both the connecting link between the two Testaments and the unifying thread that runs through the entire Bible. Here is a motif, like that of a great symphony, recurring again and again and providing the clue to the meaning of the whole. We may even say that what is new in the New Testament is not primarily a new idea of God nor a new ethic but a new beginning of the People of God.[2]

The history of the Hebrews begins with a recognition that they are a chosen people. God's word comes to Abraham, "I will make of you a great nation . . . and in you all the families of the earth will be blessed" (Gen. 12:2-3). Responding in faith, he becomes the progenitor of a people who have never ceased to believe that their history stands in a special relation to the will of God. They were God's people not because of any merit of their own but because they were to be his instrument for fulfilling his plan. In the deliverance from Egypt, God enabled them to be established as a national entity. At Sinai he

[1] Paul S. Minear, *Images of the Church in the New Testament* (Philadelphia: Westminster Press, 1960).

[2] See John Bright, *The Kingdom of God* (Richmond: John Knox Press, 1953), Chap. VII.

made a covenant with them under which they were to obey him and be "a holy nation" (Exodus 19:6). As the People of God, they had a mission to discharge in his behalf. If they were untrue to the mission, they would cease to be the true Israel of God.

Still, there would be a faithful remnant out of which would come an Israel not according to the flesh but according to the spirit (Romans 9:6-8). It is that true Israel which the early church understood itself to be. It felt itself to stand in the direct continuity between the calling of Israel and the emergence of a People of God who would come not from a single nation but "from east and west, and from north and south, and sit . . . in the Kingdom" (Luke 13:29). As the first epistle of Peter insisted, echoing the words of the covenant at Sinai, Christians are "a chosen race, a royal priesthood, a holy nation, God's own people" (I Peter 2:9).

The renewed People of God, according to St. Paul, marks the beginning of a new humanity, remade in the image of Christ, a true community of love. The old division between Jew and Gentile—or, as we would say today, between race and race, nation and nation, class and class—begins to fall away, for Christ "has broken down the dividing wall of hostility . . . that he might create in himself one new man in place of the two, so making peace" (Eph. 2:14-15).

If we lay firm hold of this picture of the church, it will be a corrective for some very superficial conceptions widely current today. One of these is that the church is just a group of individual believers who decide to come together for their spiritual nurture. This is never the biblical view. The Bible sees the church as a community created by God, who incorporates the individual into the body of his people. Another inadequate view conceives the church as only an institution. Again, this is not according to the Bible. There must, of course, be organizational forms for the perpetuation of its life and work from generation to generation, but the essential nature of the church is personal because it is always and everywhere a People.

To view the church as the People of God also emphasizes its missionary character. Israel had not been chosen for its own sake but for the sake of mankind—to proclaim faith in God and obedience to him to all the nations of the earth (Isa. 49: 5-6). That role, as St. Peter most clearly saw, was inherited by the church as the fulfiller of Israel's mission. But would it be an exaggeration to say that 90 per cent of the energy of the average parish today is directed to the private and family interests of its members? In so far as the church lives for itself instead of for the community and the world, it fails to be the People of God.

And how the picture of the church as the People of God illumines the place of the laity. They *are* the church. Yet there is all too much truth in the sardonic description of the contemporary congregation as a "frozen laity in a parson-centered institution." If the People of God is "a royal priesthood, a holy nation," then the responsibility of representing him in the world belongs not to a group of clergy but to the whole membership. To set aside certain persons, whom we label as ministers, for certain specialized functions does not relieve the others of their own varied forms of ministering. Nor is the function of the layman to be thought of as helping the clergyman in the activities that go on within the walls of the church. On the contrary, it is the function of the clergyman to help the laity in their Christian witness and service in all their daily life in society.

Still further, this conception of the church is a great impulsion to realize and manifest its unity. The People of God is one people and their fellowship in Christ is one fellowship. A

51

divided church is therefore really a contradiction in terms. We may differ as to the structural forms in which the oneness of the Christian community is to be expressed but no one who has been grasped by the biblical view can be content with our feeble manifestation of unity today. After having said everything that can be said to justify our separations, we still need to be reminded that there is only one People of God and that we have no right to obscure this reality from the world.

II

The most frequent image of the church in the New Testament is that of *The Body of Christ*. As St. Paul puts it in a classic summary for the church at Corinth, "You are the Body of Christ and individually members of it" (I Cor. 12:27).

"You are the Body of Christ": his *Body,* not just a casual collection of independent units. The church, that is to say, has an organic character, all the members being knit together in a common relation to its head. It is the community of those who, because they have fellowship with the same Lord, have a deeper fellowship with one another. The phrase, "Body of Christ," sounds so mystical that we sometimes assume it has reference only to some invisible ideal rather than to a down-to-earth actuality like a congregation on Main Street. But to St. Paul the "Body" meant the visible concrete reality by which the living Christ continues to be manifest to the world and to act in human history. Just as my physical body serves my purposes as a person, so the church as his Body is to carry on his work in the world. It is the means by which a corporate witness is to be borne and a corporate mission fulfilled.

The phrase needs also to be read with a different accent: You are "the Body of *Christ*." Not just a body of congenial neighbors or of white Americans or of citizens drawn together by idealistic interests, but "of Christ." Here in the church, in other words, is something that *we* do not create. It owes its existence to Christ, not to any human design. It can never be true to itself, therefore, if it merely reflects the views of those who happen to be its members at any point of time. It is really the church only when it represents Christ. It fails to be the church if it proclaims only what people like to hear or adjusts its witness to the level of popular favor.

Many a congregation, however, feels toward the church too much like the Texas rancher who wanted to establish on his own broad acres everything that could contribute to making an agreeable community. So he built a school, a library, a recreation center, and finally a beautiful chapel. A visitor asked, "Mr. Rancher, do you belong to this church?" "Why, no," he replied, "this church belongs to me." We shall never lay hold of the full significance of the church until we understand that it belongs not to us but to Christ, and that it is his purpose, not our preferences, that determine what it should be and do.

The more faithful the church is to its true nature as the Body of Christ, the more likely will there be tension between it and a non-Christian or sub-Christian world. The tension may be creative, even though it is uncomfortable and we try to relieve it by tranquilizers. One of the most common tranquilizers in a church is to limit the lordship of Christ to the more intimate personal affairs, and not claim it over the complex social and economic and political relationships. It is still possible, for example, for a church to take the same kind of tranquilizer that the Methodist Episcopal Church South took in 1858 when it carefully kept its ban on dancing and cardplaying but removed the ban on owning slaves.

Another way in which the church may take a tranquilizer is

to be silent in the presence of contemporary tensions between itself and secular society. But by conforming to its cultural environment, the church loses its power to change the environment. We had a tragic illustration of this in the case of the German churches under the Nazi regime. When we witness today the dramatic production of "The Deputy," it is easy to see how the failure of Pope Pius XII to take an open stand against Hitler's treatment of the Jews kept him from truly filling the role of one who was called the Vicar of Christ. It is not so easy to recognize defections in our own American churches as representatives of Christ. There are plenty of congregations that would be shocked to be told that by being racially exclusive or taking no stand on civil rights for Negro as well as white they are failing to be the church of him who has broken down "the dividing wall of hostility" that he might "reconcile us both to God in one body through the cross" (Eph. 2:14, 16).

Beyond all else, however, we must remember that by preserving the vision of Christ, the church provides the criterion for its own self-criticism. It is the one institution which has within itself the constant source of its own reformation. For at the originative center of its life there is the figure of Jesus Christ as the standard by which everything else in its life is to be judged. It may become bogged down in the ruts of routine and inertia into which all institutions tend to sink, but always at the fountainhead of its existence there is the life-giving Spirit which brought the church into being at Pentecost. It is this innate capacity for renewal that makes the church the miracle of history.

CHRISTIANITY TAKES TO THE STREETS

by EDWIN T. DAHLBERG

Crozer Theological Seminary, Chester, Pa.;
Former President, National Council of Churches

ACTS 2:6-8

The nearest I have ever come to the Pentecostal experience of speaking in tongues was in November, 1961, one week before the opening of the Third Assembly of the World Council of Churches in New Delhi, India.

The occasion was a denominational rather than an interdenominational one. It celebrated the 125th Anniversary Jubilee of our Baptist work in Northeast India, at Gauhati, Assam. Six thousand delegates from eighteen tribal groups—Nagas, Garos, and other hill tribes who were only one or two generations removed from a head-hunting culture—were crowded together in the vast open air bamboo and palm leaf tabernacle called a *pandal*. Some of them, particularly the various Naga groups, had to have a police permit to attend because of the restless, insurgent conditions prevailing in the jungles of Assam at the time.

Rarely have I witnessed such a colorful scene. Each delegation had come in ceremonial costume, with spears, shields, ivory or wooden armlets, and brightly bespangled ornamentation of every kind. Probably half of them were young people. It was a tremendous vindication of the world mission of the Christian church.

Seated on the grassy floor of the tabernacle, this multitude of believers was divided into twelve linguistic sections, each with its own interpreter. As I preached to them, a paragraph at a time, the interpreters rose to their feet and began to interpret simultaneously the gospel message, each in his own tongue. They spoke with fiery power and intensity, with dramatic gestures and passionate pleading, as those seated closely around them listened eagerly. Rarely have I felt such a sense of Pentecostal re-enforcement and joy in my preaching, as I heard the gospel coming back to me in so many tongues, in a kind of New Testament excitement and enthusiasm.

This was not literally the kind of speaking with tongues we read about in the book of Acts or in Paul's letter to the Corinthians (I Cor. 14:1-19), which, in the Greek New Testament, is called the miracle of *glossolalia*. This latter phenomenon, though beyond our understanding and attended with many cautious warnings by the apostle Paul, has had a revival of interest in various church circles of our own time. It is deserving of respectful study, too, for we cannot doubt that many Christians have had their hearts revitalized and reborn as a result of the Pentecostalist movement.

Nevertheless, by reason of the danger and confusion Paul describes as so often attending the speaking with tongues in the New Testament congregations, I prefer to think of Pentecost in terms of what I saw and heard in Assam: the universal language of the good news of God in Jesus Christ, so interpreted by love that the people of every nation, tribe, and tongue can understand it.

The excitement and joy of this universal language of the Holy Spirit I think we all felt again at New Delhi the week following, when Christian believers from 90 different nations and some 200 branches of the Protestant and Eastern Orthodox and other communions came together in the beautiful Vigyan Bhavan—the civic auditorium of New Delhi—in the historic Third Assembly of the World Council of Churches. Though the messages there were amplified by all the electronic devices of our modern microphonic translation systems—in English, German, French, Spanish, and Russian—we felt the same spirit of Christian unity and mission, especially when we repeated the Lord's Prayer together in all the major languages of mankind, or sang together the inspired resurrection hymn:

> Thine be the glory,
> Risen, conqu'ring Son!

Is Pentecost reproducible?

It is reproducible—probably in some different modern form —if we think in terms of the preparations that preceded it.

This preparation involved, first of all, a hopeful and expectant waiting upon God. There were only about 120 disciples to begin with, who assembled for prayer in an upper room somewhere in Jerusalem, in obedience to the injunction of Jesus that they should "wait for the promise of the Father," namely, the baptism of the Holy Spirit (Acts 1:4-5).

As Theodore P. Ferris has pointed out in his comment on this verse, there is room for passivity as well as activity in the life of man. We can *work* for a living; we can only *wait* for the spring.[1] [Italics mine.]

These early Christians were waiting for the spring—a melting visitation from on high. They looked for spiritual rivers

[1] Theodore P. Ferris, "The Book of Acts," *The Interpreter's Bible* (Nashville: Abingdon Press, 1954), IX, 27.

running full again, for trees budding and bursting into foliage, for the ridges becoming soft with showers, for birds singing their mating calls. We may have to wait thus again, in a time when the fields of the kingdom are hard as stone, when hearts are frozen, when opposing classes, races, and nations look at each other across the bargaining table with the icy stares of the cold war.

When Jesus told his followers to wait for the Spirit of God and the promise of the Father, he knew all too well that, without the accumulated reserves of faith, courage, and love that come from God alone, they would not be equal to the tests ahead. This is why it is so important in the home and in the church that we should address ourselves to prayer, whether in family worship and personal devotions, in cell group meditation and study, or in the public prayer meetings of the congregation. It should be something more than an exercise in stilted liturgy and ritual. There should be a return to the warm, spontaneous, voluntary sharing of Christian experience that was characteristic of our fathers, but which all too many of us have lost in an age that has almost completely substituted activity for quietness, and convention addresses for contemplation.

Dr. Karl Menninger of the Menninger Foundation, in an address at Chautauqua, N.Y., July 17, 1964, made some very significant statements about the attitude of the public both toward the mentally disturbed and toward the criminally inclined. He said that hope is as important as love. "Our difficulty in dealing with mental patients, and with criminals, too," he declared, "is not so much that we are helpless, as that we are hopeless."

This is the problem of the Christian church today. We feel helpless because we have become so hopeless. We hear so much said about the post-Christian era and the irrelevance of the church that we have become almost psychopathic in our absorption with our ailments. Devoutly to be desired is the day—and may it come soon—when all our talk about irrelevance will become irrelevant. The gospel of Jesus Christ, bravely lived and proclaimed, is still the best hope of mankind. Once we become saturated with that hope we will no longer be so helpless. For this to happen we need the quiet waiting, thinking, self-examination, praying, and ruminating upon the will of God that stilled the little company meeting in the upper room. Only so can we reproduce the miracle of Pentecost.

There is a danger here, however. People often resort to prayer as an evasion. How often we hear the superficial suggestion, "If we would only pray more, there would be no problem." Thus do we dodge great moral issues, fail in our evangelistic and missionary witness, and betray our stewardship, while piously and hypocritically watching whole nations go to their doom. Charles G. Finney, the eloquent evangelist of the nineteenth century who later became the president of Oberlin, was possessed of keen spiritual insight when he said that "revivals must be *worked up* as well as *prayed down*."

The handful of believers who prayed together in the upper room while waiting for the promise of the Father, were also very practical people. They knew that "life is a strange mixture of rapture and routine, and we cannot have one without the other."[2] So they proceeded to develop an organization. Peter called for an election, and nominations for someone to take the place of Judas in the apostolate of the twelve. Barsabbas and Matthias were nominated. By a process of prayer combined with the ancient method of voting by the casting of lots, Matthias was elected. The church had an organized leadership, and was ready for its mission.

[2] *Ibid.*, p. 34.

Many church people—and this is true of people in all community agencies—profess a kind of scorn for organization. How many worthy projects have been defeated by someone getting up and repeating the old cliché, "It looks as if we are getting over-organized—too many wheels within wheels."

The trouble is not that we are over-organized. Rather it is that we are poorly and inefficiently organized, with too few people involved in the church's mission. Those who talk about wheels within wheels would be well advised to look up that passage from the book of Ezekiel in the Old Testament (Ezek. 1:1-28). They would find that in his graphic vision the prophet saw the effective functioning of the Holy Spirit within the wheels in perfect co-ordination. The wheels were rimmed with jewels, flashing and sparkling in the sun. Wherever the spirit was to go, the wheels went also. From the movement of the wheels and the wings of the living creatures came a sound as of great waters, "like the thunder of the Almighty, a sound of tumult like the sound of a host." Over this entire vision was spread the glory of the Lord. And the spirit that was in the wheels and in the living creatures entered into Ezekiel, so that he was prepared to receive and obey the call of God.

Let us remember this the next time we hear people speaking contemptuously of organization. The church needs a structure as well as a spirit. Indeed, the structure—the efficiency and harmony of the administrative process—may be the condition of receiving the spirit. There would never have been the spirit of Christian unity that we have in the ecumenical movement today—the climate of understanding and good will now moving across the world—had it not been for the organization and structure made available for the Holy Spirit through the National and World Councils of Churches of the Protestant and

Eastern Orthodox communions, and the Vatican Council of the Roman Catholic faith.

There are a great many wheels in these organizations, and wheels within wheels, too. But the spirit is in the wheels—evangelizing, witnessing, and serving on every continent of the globe. Spiritual unity without institutional unity is all too often a ghost without a body. We should thank God, therefore, that in the local, state, national, and international organizations of the ecumenical movement the unity for which Christ prayed is becoming a visible, working unity. We are coming nearer to the Pentecostal situation described in the book of Acts, where we read of the disciples that "they were all together in one place" (Acts 2:1). This happened *after* they were organized, not before.

One thing remains to be done, if we are to reproduce the experience of Pentecost. *Christianity must take to the streets.*

How many of the three thousand that were added to the church on the day of Pentecost would have heard the gospel and been converted if the preaching of Peter and the testimony of the believers had been confined to the little congregation of 120 people in the upper room? Probably very few. It was because they went out among the people that things began to happen.

Evidences are multiplying everywhere that the churches are adopting the Pentecostal method. Content no longer with a walled-in religion, barricaded behind pulpits, choir rails, altar rails, and stained glass windows, God's people are once more taking to the streets, confronting the multitude with the life and message of Jesus Christ.

This is going further than the use of the mass media. While we may well rejoice that evangelists, preachers, pastors, and missionaries are reaching millions of people by means of the radio channels, television, motion picture films, and the public press, something even more significant is happening now: a face to face confrontation with people where they live and work and do business.

A notable example was the freedom march on Washington during the summer of 1963, when whites and Negroes together converged on the capital city in an orderly demonstration for civil rights. To be sure, this was not the preaching of the gospel as such. But it was a spiritual movement that shook the moral conscience of the nation. And it has set the pattern which we ought to follow in all our witnessing for Christ. As long as we stay in our church sanctuaries, or radio and TV studios, we do not make an adequate personal impact.

We were all reminded of this in one of the sectional meetings on evangelism in the Evanston Assembly of the World Council of Churches in 1954, when the head of religious programming for the British Broadcasting Corporation warned us that even the most effective radio or TV speaker would have little power to change people religiously unless there was a follow-up the next day by women talking over the back fence to their neighbors, or business men to their associates in the office, and asking the question, "What did you think of that religious program on TV last night?" The person-to-person, eyeball-to-eyeball encounter of the Christian with the non-believing world is still the most powerful form of witnessing for Christ. This is what Jesus had in mind when he sent the twelve into the surrounding villages, saying, *"Preach as you go"* (Matt. 10:7).

It has been my privilege during the forty-five years of my active ministry to preach many times in churches, meeting halls, and radio and TV stations. But in none of these experiences have I had quite the same sense of being baptized into a feeling of the people, as John Woolman expressed it, as in the various street demonstrations in which I have taken part this past year. One occasion was a racial demonstration in Chester, Pennsylvania. Another was participation in the Silent Vigil of the theological students of America across from the Lincoln Memorial in Washington, D.C., during the Senate debate on the civil rights bill, while a group of Nazis demonstrated a few yards away with the sign, "America For White Christians Only."

But the day that imparted to me most vividly the sense of Pentecost was the Pentecost Sunday afternoon in Philadelphia, May 17, 1964, when the Society of Friends and other peace groups of that city marched silently through the downtown streets in a "Christian Walk for Peace." Some three hundred people walked quietly for nearly two hours in orderly procession, obeying the signal lights and all the laws, and holding high various banners with such slogans as "BREAD NOT BOMBS," "BLESSED ARE THE PEACE-MAKERS," and quotations from the Bible and from the papal encyclical, "Pacem in Terris" ("Peace on Earth"). Block by block, two men on each side of the street passed out literature to the passers-by and to the people sitting on the apartment house front steps along the way. Thousands of automobiles slowed up in order to read the signs and to receive the literature. At half a dozen of the leading downtown churches we stopped for a five minute rest period, and in each instance the pastors and some of their laymen spoke a word of friendly greeting or led us in prayer.

No one would contend that this was the preaching of the gospel in the sense that Peter preached it on the first day of Pentecost. But it was a public witness in behalf of a faith. And whether it was a silent vigil for civil rights at the Lincoln Memorial or a Christian Walk for Peace in Philadelphia, it was most impressive to see the number of people reached with the message. Essentially this is what we must do in preaching the gospel—take to the streets in one form or another. We can not remain in retreats and ivory towers forever. It is heartening to know of the way in which the department of evangelism of the National Council of Churches is now reaching the millions of people who swarm into our national parks each summer, with worship services that stretch all the way from the Grand Canyon to Alaska, and to the ski slopes east and west. The local church will always be the permanent worship and witnessing center. But in this age of movement and mobility we must follow people where they are, even to ships at sea, and to factories, offices, farms, high-rise apartments, hospitals, and jails. This means that not only the ordained ministers, but the laymen in their vocations, must preach as they go, incorporating the good news of God in Jesus Christ into every phase of human life. And we must do it boldly.

A friend of mine who is the pastor of a large Negro congregation suffered, in his youth, from a serious impediment in his speech that caused him to stammer unmercifully. A school inspector on St. Kitt's Island said to him one day, "You must conquer this, or you will be handicapped all your life. Here's what I want you to do. Memorize some of the great passages from the Bible, the plays of Shakespeare, and the addresses of Abraham Lincoln. Then go down and stand on the banks of the river. Sense the flow and freedom of it—catch the rhythm of it. Go down, too, to the ocean. Listen to the winds, and to the waves, and to the tides—the music and the power of the sea. Then SPEAK! *SPEAK* to the greatness of it!"

This my friend did month after month, year after year. Little wonder that he is today a great preacher of the gospel, and that, in addition, he can hold his hearers spellbound by the hour, as he recites to them the immortal words of the Scriptures, of Shakespeare, of Lincoln, and Demosthenes.

We are suffering today in the churches from a critical impediment in our speech. As we face this terrible world we stammer in the preaching of the gospel. Now is the time to listen to the rivers of history, and to catch the music and the rhythm of their flow; to hearken to the Word of God; to feel the shock and foaming tumult of the vast tides of the Spirit rolling in from the Eternal; to wait for the promises of the Father. And then, in the name of God, to speak to the greatness of our time—SPEAK, concerning the Christ who died for all. For who knows but what Pentecost is at hand?

THE GIFT OF TONGUES

by ROBERT I. GANNON, S. J.

Superior, Jesuit Missions House,
New York, N.Y.

This morning in flaming vestments we sing the Mass of the Fiery Tongues—the Mass of Pentecost; a Mass of great beauty for a feast of great dignity; the only feast of the year that ranks liturgically with Easter; the feast which, in a sense, celebrates the birthday of the church.

It is true that our Lord had outlined the future activities of his apostles before he ascended into heaven. He had taught them the essential truths, had established the sacraments and had himself offered the first holy sacrifice beginning in the supper room and ending on Calvary.

But all this spiritual force, to be known for the rest of time as his church, lay, as it were, in a trance until the Paraclete should come. The living voice of the church was silent. Her eyes were held. Her sacramental hands and the blessed gospel feet that were to tramp the far-flung highways of the world were motionless. The apostles cowered with fear behind the closed doors of an upper room till "suddenly there came a sound from heaven as of a mighty wind coming and it filled the whole house where they were sitting and there appeared to them parted tongues as it were of fire and it sat upon every one of them and they were filled with the Holy Spirit."

Then, like an intricate piece of mechanism when the power is suddenly turned on and wheels and rods and pistons and bolts began to move, or better, perhaps, like a sleeping man who stirs himself and wakes to action, the church began at once to teach; began the exercise of a duty and a power most offensive to the world then and now and always; offensive by its assumption of authority, but more offensive still in its message. Its message that day was the message that has been repeated every day and hour since, because the church has only one sermon to preach. The church, like St. Paul, is satisfied to know "only Christ and him crucified," "a stumbling-block to Jews and folly to Gentiles."

So on that first Pentecostal morning the apostles went out into the market place to preach not only Christ—they had done that while he was still on earth—but him crucified and risen, and as they preached a most significant miracle occurred. For the words these simple Galileans spoke were understood by every man in the crowd, each in his own language—Egyptian, Greek, and Aramaic. From the Holy Spirit had come the gift of tongues, and the church that day was preaching the same sermon to men of every sort and condition, but preaching in a language that everyone could understand. Everyone that witnessed the miracle marveled then, and everyone may marvel just as well today.

The church still has the gift of tongues, still speaks to the whole human race, to the simple and the learned, the rich and the poor, the weak and the strong of every nation on the face of the earth; still preaches the same sermon, but unfortunately it is not always understood. It is true that when the church speaks now or in any age the message comes from her soul, that is, from Christ, who can always speak to all his people with clarity, authority, and power. But the lips and breath and teeth and tongue of the church are human, and its human element has been responsible for endless confusion and division. The tenth century had its problems, the sixteenth century had more numerous and more complicated ones, and now the twentieth century has such ominous problems that those who were separated from one another in the tenth and sixteenth centuries are being drawn together again. We are facing the common and universal danger of a world-wide atheism that aims at the destruction of all religion.

One of the few bright lights on the horizon is the spirit of discussion that is spreading amongst us—a discussion without any of the bitterness that characterized the vicious debates of the past. This is the era of what we call the "dialogue"—an old word with a new meaning. It means that Protestants and Catholics are getting together now as fellow Christians; getting together to clear the air and look for points of agreement. When we talk about religious unity, it is very far from any thought of indifferentism. We do not believe that one religion is just as good as another and we hope that nobody else does either. Everyone should be able to feel that his own is the best one— the best one for him to follow.

What we want is the spirit of the men who settled the state of Maryland, Leonard Calvert and the Protestants and Catholics who came over with him in the *Ark* and the *Dove*. Drawing up their first charter, they drew up the first charter of religious liberty in the new world. In it we read these words—remarkable in the bitter old seventeenth century: "Every man might be of what religion he pleased and might endeavor to draw others to it by the force of argument and by amicable and modest words, but without bitterness against others who might have other opinions."

This ideal spread gradually from Maryland to the rest of the United States so that today the various forms of religion practiced in our pluralistic homeland are so numerous that in these few moments we must confine ourselves to a comparatively small group: to what we call practical or devout Christians. The indifferent, fallen-away type have watered down their beliefs in such a way that too often we have very little in common.

Practical Christians, on the other hand, share with one another not only the Old Testament with its one true God and the Ten Commandments—this we share with the Jews as well and to a degree with the Mohammedans—but the New Testament with all the implications involved in the mystery of the Holy Trinity. We all believe that the promises made in the Old Testament were fulfilled in the New. We believe that the Messiah has come; that the Old Testament is ended. We all say the Apostles Creed and we declare our belief "in Jesus Christ, His Only Son, Our Lord who was conceived of the Holy Ghost and born of the Virgin Mary." We all see in Christ not only a teacher, not only a prophet, not only the best man who ever lived, as some people call him, not only a brother and a friend but the Second Person of the Blessed Trinity, true God and true Man. This is a tremendous bond, more important than anything that separates us.

When we go on in the recitation of the Creed and come to the words "I believe in the Holy catholic Church," Protestants mean one thing and Catholics another. For most Protestants, the catholic church is an invisible body made up of all who believe in Christ. For the Catholic it is a visible body established as such by Christ and endowed with the power to rule in spiritual matters and teach without fear of error. That is an important difference, of course, but the fact remains that we are all saying the same Creed.

There is difference, too, with regard to the number of sacraments, but we share the desire for the sacraments. So with the communion of saints and the forgiveness of sins, there are differences with regard to what constitutes a saint and the necessity of auricular confession, but when we discuss these things there is no confusion of tongues. We have so much to build on.

The first time I visited the University of Alabama for a Spiritual Orientation Week, I faced a 90 per cent Protestant audience with a dozen Protestant clergymen in the front row. At the end, a venerable Methodist minister held out his hand and said: "I had no idea, Reverend, that a Roman Catholic priest could preach such a good Methodist sermon." It was not a Methodist sermon, of course. It was a Christian sermon on the meaning of life. The point was that my Methodist friend thought that a sermon, to be Catholic, had to concern itself with miracles, visions, and private revelations. It is true that we believe in these things. "The hand of the Lord is not shortened" and he can still do anything he did in the time of Moses. But there are so many other things to preach about when you have as your general subject Christ and him crucified—so many things that strike a sympathetic note everywhere, especially in an ecumenical age.

In this connection, see how the Bible is being studied now in all the better seminaries. Future ministers and priests are not interested any longer in using Holy Scripture as a club to subdue other Christians. They are not looking up trick references that can be fashioned into arguments. They are trying to understand the text as it was intended to be understood from the very beginning. They are asking themselves what was originally written and what did the author mean exactly when he wrote it? What is the precise modern equivalent? So that now there is a project afoot to have Catholic scholars and Protestant scholars and Jewish scholars collaborate on an English text that will be acceptable to all.

This is most appropriate in a pluralistic society like ours. Pluralistic? This is another old word with a new meaning and the new meaning is this: a society in which many faiths freely exist; one in which religious rights are freely guaranteed to all. Our own United States was never anything else. It was never Protestant, though the majority of its citizens might be Protestant. It was never Catholic, never Jewish. It was, from the beginning, free for everybody. But what makes the theory of pluralism a practical ideal is the charity that all children of God must feel toward other children of God because they are children of God. When good Pope John recently called together an Ecumenical Council he established as one of its principal purposes "to make clear to everyone that each and every person is our brother and our friend." He referred, of course, to every son of Adam, but first and foremost to every fellow Christian.

Racial stock with its common language of the lips had never been too successful in creating universal charity. Blood may be thicker than water, but it is not thick enough to cement the human race unless it be the blood of Christ. For what is the only thing that keeps on sending, all through the ages of the church, thousands of men and women, intellectual, well-bred men and women, out into the back alleys and jungles of the world to sacrifice themselves for strange human beings without a semblance of even physical appeal; to pour out their love upon them as they would upon their own? It is certainly not philology or family pride. It is not the fact that the savages in Umzila's kraal have a word that sounds like "uncle" or tribal customs that seem to link them to Leviticus and the wandering Jews. It is the simpler and much more mysterious fact that the missionary can hold one of Christ's wounded hands and the savage can hold the other; that they can be brothers not so much in Adam as in Christ.

For Christ wants both of them as his brothers, not only as his Father's fellow creatures. That was why he told his apostles and their successors to leave no part of the world unvisited. All nations were to be baptized. All were to be regenerated by the sacrament and all the men and women and little children made co-heirs with him. Thus the old disciple and the new could both partake with him of the same divine nature. Both could claim an equal share in the heritage of adoption—of a unique adoption never known before or since.

For every other adoption that we know is a legal fiction which leaves the nature of the child unchanged. So that if a European were to adopt an Eskimo or an African, the children would still be of different parentage though linked by a piece of paper. It is only a divine adoption that penetrates to the inner core, renovating the soul, enriching it, transforming it into the likeness of Jesus Christ himself. So that it is the inner life that draws us closer together rather than the outer. It is our adoption rather than our racial ties; it is the language of the heart rather than the language of the lips.

72

As Christians we have found this common language of the heart. In praying as we do for ultimate success we have found a common denominator first of all in the fatherhood of God. This is one prayer which can come with sincerity from the heart of every practical Christian. Many sincere good men cannot say the "Hail Mary" of the Angel Gabriel because "Grace" gives them difficulty and divine maternity is too much and they don't believe in angels anyway. The sacrifice of the Mass, with all its beauty and majesty, supposing as it does a Catholic attitude and tradition, is out of the question for many, incomprehensible except for one short part. Midway between the Consecration and the Communion the celebrant robed symbolically as another Christ, with hands outstretched in the ancient way, repeats a prayer word for word as it fell from the lips of our Lord: "Our Father, Who art in Heaven." That strikes a chord of universal harmony. For the Lord's Prayer is shared by many outside of Christendom itself. How much more it should mean to us.

If Christians can be united to pray to one Father as a Father, they will someday be praying with other Christians as brothers in Christ. The one supposes and complements the other. For just as modern philanthropy is a withered barren thing when it works for the brotherhood of man and ignores the fatherhood of God, so a religion is perverse which goes no farther than the fatherhood of God and fails to emphasize the brotherhood of man: a brotherhood that springs from no mere accident of lineage running back to Africa, if that was the cradle of the human race, but a strong bond sealed with the blood of Christ.

Let men but recognize that bond and mutual hate will change to a sympathetic interest. This, in turn, will mean a sharing of ideals, a spiritual union that will know one Shepherd. If just those souls that should be Christian will breathe in a thousand dialects of the lips this single aspiration of the heart: "Our Father, who art in heaven, hallowed by thy name, thy kingdom come, thy will be done on earth as it is in heaven," then all can say: "We have heard others speak in our own tongue, the wonderful works of God."

GOD'S PLACE, PURPOSE, AND PEOPLE

by KYLE HASELDEN

Editor, The *Christian Century*

I PETER 2:1-10

One of the young men who belonged to a church I served for several years was a recent and somewhat reluctant convert from another church. He used to bring his small daughter into the sanctuary of our Baptist temple and in a hushed tone say to her, "This is God's house; this is where God lives." I was not surprised when, after some months, he returned to his earlier church and, at that, not to the best, but to the most primitive, form of that church's belief about God's habitation. It did surprise me that a man so much concerned about God's house should abandon his wife and child on his way from one church to another. I was convinced then, and still am, that there is a direct connection between a man's will to keep God in a specific, restricted place and that same man's moral irresponsibility.

I.

What is God's house? Where is God's place? George Bernard Shaw once said, "Beware of the man whose God is in heaven." Indeed so! Beware of the man who houses his God exclusively in any specific place, whether in heaven or on earth. Beware of the man whose God is *there* but not *here, then* but not *now, sometimes* but not *always*. Beware of the man who has a household god which can be taken with him or left behind, a god so small that he thinks it can be taken out of the schools or put into the schools by the judicial or legislative acts of men. Beware of the man who thinks he can capture the King of the Universe in a theological formula, or hold that infinite God by a text from the Bible or put that boundless God in a creed, dogma, or doctrine. Most of all, beware of the man who believes that the church is God's house, that the church is the place where God lives. Said the apostle Paul, "The God who made the world and everything in it, being Lord of heaven and earth, does not live in shrines made by men."

What is God's place? Before going to the Second Session of Vatican Council II in Rome, I thought it well to read some brief but solid book on Protestantism. After all, when a Baptist surrenders himself to the charm of the Eternal City he wants to be sure that he will return no less a Protestant than when he went. I found what I needed in a paperback reprint of a thirty-five-year-old book by the German theologian Karl Heim, a book called *The Nature of Protestantism.* Heim believed that the Protestant Reformation destroyed the ancient, anti-Christian concept of the temple as a sacred precinct and that when this temple was destroyed the whole world became the temple of God.

What is God's place? Heim answers with Luther that God's place is the workshop, the office, the kitchen, the street, the field, the sea, the slum, and perhaps even the church. In a beautifully tender passage Heim wrote: "In every place the world is impure, in the monastery as well as outside of it; and in every place it may be the throne of grace, the non-spatial realm in which God comes near to us and in which the Christ is invisibly

76

present and accessible. His gracious presence is omnipresent and cannot be confined to a eucharistic tabernacle: 'Foxes have holes and birds of the air have nests; but the Son of Man has nowhere to lay his head.' Christ wanders homeless through the centuries. He is nowhere and everywhere."[1] I had read that text numerous times but had never seen it as I see it now. Our Lord's poverty— no place to lay his head—became his abundance, for he is everywhere and in all times at home! And where Christ is, God is: "God was in Christ reconciling the world to himself."

If the world is God's place, if that is where God is, what, then, is the world? One of the tragedies of Protestantism is its drifting back into a pre-Reformation definition of the world. We tend to view the world which "God so loved" and into which the Risen Christ sent his disciples in geographic rather than in psychological and social terms. This view has fostered foreign missions but it has simultaneously discouraged social action. So we send missionaries to convert Negroes in Africa but exclude converted Negroes from our lives in America. We have mistaken the earth for the world and missionary scope for redemptive thoroughness.

What is the world? The most prosaic dictionary definition will do as well as any. Webster's Collegiate Dictionary defines the world as: 1. The earth and the heavens.—So, wherever we go spatially that is where God is. The Russian cosmonaut did not see God when he circled the globe for the simple reason that he had not seen God before he circled the globe. 2. The dictionary defines the world as "the earth and its inhabitants, with their affairs and interests—hence humanity, mankind, also people in general, the public."

This is the world into which God came when Christ was

[1] Karl Heim, *The Nature of Protestantism* (Philadelphia: Fortress Press, 1963), p. 137.

born of Mary—not to the earth but into humanity; into its agonies and fears and pains, into its hopes and joys and questing struggles, into man's clashing ideas and blending aspirations. Thus the shame of that Bethlehem inn too crowded for the Christ child: The Lord of the universe came humbly as an infant guest and was refused. Thus the shame of our too-busy lives which reject a wandering Christ and in the act exclude the proprietor of all habitations. "He came unto his own"—they belonged to him—"and his own received him not."

God's place is the world and the world is man and all his affairs. God has no far-off cosmic residence which does not include your home, no vineyard which does not include your little vine, no place from which the rights of private property permit you to withhold the lot on which you live, the ground on which you work and play, and the grave in which you will be buried. You have no enterprise sealed against his intrusion, no secret thoughts, no private affairs. God's place is wherever God wills to be and he wills to be in the world.

II.

If the world is God's place, what is his purpose in that place? As a teacher of young seminarians and the editor of a journal of preaching, I encounter over and over again all the old sermon outlines and the cute sermon titles. One of the clever titles, which apparently and perhaps fortunately the young ministers have overlooked, raises our second question: "What in heaven's name is God doing on earth?" Yes, what is God's purpose in his place? What God is doing elsewhere in the universe is so far beyond our comprehension that it is probably blasphemous even to ask about it. But what is he doing here? That question has its total answer in one man, Jesus Christ.

Time and again Jesus said of his ministry: "I came that . . . " and ended this saying in such a variety of ways that even listing them would exhaust our time. Is there a short cut? a summary? a peg or two on which to hang Christ's whole ministry?

There are at least two clues, the first in John 8:36: "So if the Son makes you free, you will be free indeed." God wants his children to be free. He sent his Son as Redeemer to pay his people's bond and strike their chains when they drift into slavery, to overthrow the oppressor and release the oppressed. God's cry in Egypt echoes in every age and in every land where his people are in any way enslaved: "Let my people go!" God came in Christ to claim his children as his own, overthrowing their slavish devotion to anything that is not God.

Think how much of all that is precious to us is caught up in that one word "Free." Forgiveness, liberating us from the exhausting weight of sin and guilt; health, releasing our minds and bodies from consuming sickness and nagging pain; knowledge and truth, unshackling minds chained by ignorance, superstition, and bigotry; life, rolling the stones from before our graves and letting us fly into the Father's arms; hope and faith, putting fear to rout and shielding us from fear's intimidation. Let the mind catalogue the heart's desires and you will be amazed to discover how much of the richness and joy of life defines itself in freedom's language: health, peace, plenty, wisdom, knowledge, confidence, holiness, faith, identity—each of these requires freedom as its indispensable ingredient.

So God came in Christ to liberate his children. It grieves him to see his children slaves to foul thoughts and craven deeds, burdened by their sin and tormented by guilt. It grieves him to see his majestic creature hobbled by ignorance, fear, superstition, and hatred. It grieves him when the people are oppressed by poverty, hunger, and disease. And it grieves him even more when wily men intimidate, oppress, and exploit other men. Throughout the Bible, from one end of it to the other, there is no divine cry more constant than the cry in Egypt: "Let my people go!" And in Christ, God's demand that his children be free took the ultimate instrumental form and became flesh that through his Son we may be free indeed.

Is this all God is doing? Is this his whole purpose in this place? No, there is a second clue, John 17:20-21: "I do not pray for these only, but also for those who are to believe in me through their word, that they may all be one; even as thou Father, art in me, and I in thee, that they also may be in us, so that the world may believe that thou has sent me." God wants his children to be one. This is dangerous ground and we must walk over it carefully. We are tempted to believe that oneness demands sameness, to insist that we cannot have unity without having uniformity. But sameness is evidently not the purpose of God. He is too busy creating diversity to be concerned about likeness. No two things in all his creation are exactly alike. What God wants for his children is a community of differences: several races but one blood; many churches but one Church; varied tongues but one understanding; many nations but one world; many temperaments, interests, skills but one unifying love. When a powerful magnet is brought into play on a field of iron filings, it instantly orders all the filings in a definite pattern. Each iron filing retains its separate identity but all of them are given their proper relationship to each other and to the central power. So the spirit of God wills to work upon the fragmentary and varied parts of human society. This is the meaning of the Pentecost event. It is not his purpose to melt down the differences and weld one unvarying social order. It is his purpose to give to each its proper relationship to the other and to all, their proper relationship to him. This is the oneness God wants for human society.

Note, then, how the freedom and the oneness God wants for man place each other in tension. God wants for us a kind of polarity of good things: singleness and solidarity, diversity and unity, personality and communion. The freedom that God wants for man cannot be libertinism, for that kind of license disrupts the unity of society; it cannot be arrogant, for arrogance alienates one man from the other; it cannot be irresponsible, for liberty without responsibility is anarchy; it cannot be exclusive, for special privilege for one man always means deprivation for some other man. The unity that God wants for man cannot be uniformity, for uniformity prohibits freedom. It cannot be politically coerced, for the affections and loyalties of a free man cannot be regimented by force. Freedom and oneness must coexist, complement, and fulfill one another. They must hold each other in tension. And that tension in any one of us or in any group of us is too great for merely human controls. Therefore God sent his Son to "reconcile the world unto himself" that each of us might be in that Christ a free moral agent—a person—and that all of us might in Christ have community.

Walking among us and addressing each of us individually the spirit of Jesus Christ says, "I want you to be *you* and I am here to redeem you from every slavery which cramps your noblest powers, to strike the chains which manacle your hands and feet, to bless every effort in my spirit to untie the oppressive fetters by which men bind men. I am your redeemer come to set you free." Then, addressing all of us together he says, "I want you to be *one* and I am here to throw across the lines of your division and conflict the uniting ties of my spirit, that you,

81

remaining many, may be one." This is what God is doing in the world, his purpose in this place. He is creating that beautiful, splendid, miraculous thing: a person. And he is calling persons into that equally beautiful, splendid, miraculous thing: community.

III.

If this is God's purpose in this place, who are God's people? At a coffee break the other day I was telling our staff how difficult it is to get young ministers to use some variety in introducing the reading of the Scripture. Almost without exception the young ministers say, "The Scripture for today is taken from . . ." Surely there must be some other way to announce God's Holy Word. The members of the staff tried their hand at devising various ways to announce the Scripture. We gave first prize for wittiness to one of the secretaries who said, "For variety the minister should say before reading the Scripture, 'And now, a word from our sponsor!'" We had our chuckle but it occurred to me afterward that in this suggestion there is a deep and appropriate wisdom. For God does sponsor a people to secure his purpose in this place.

Christians are not merely God's children; they are also his people. I Peter 2:9 reads: "But you are a chosen race, a royal priesthood, a holy nation, God's own people. . ." Who are the chosen people? It is apparent from Scripture that God's chosen people are those who choose to be chosen. Who are the adult members of God's family? Who bears the family likeness? Those who do the will of God, those who seek among men the purposes he seeks. In his early ministry when his strange deeds and extraordinary words raised questions about his sanity, Jesus' mother and brethren came to take him home. Informed

82

of their presence outside the house Jesus said, "Who is my mother, or my brethren? And he looked around about on them which sat about him, and said, Behold my mother and my brethren! For whosoever shall do the will of God, the same is my brother, and my sister, and mother."

To be a kinsman of Jesus Christ is to share the nature of Christ; and it is the nature of Christ to seek the purposes of the Father. If we are indifferent to our fellow men, deny them justice, find in their plight excuses to cheat and oppress them; if we lie, steal, and bear false witness; if we exploit, exclude, and ignore our fellowmen, we are not the chosen people. However deep the water in which we were baptized, however unbroken the succession of Sundays at public worship, we are not "a royal priesthood," if we boorishly or genteelly ignore God's purpose in this place.

Jesus Christ needs a people, a royal priesthood, a family. He needs next of kin: brothers who bear with him the burdens of mankind, sisters who sense with him the ache and grief of a weary world, and men and women who will be his mother, every day bringing him to life in a world in which every day he dies. That word from I Peter—there was more to it: "But you are a chosen race, a royal priesthood, a holy nation, God's own people, that you may declare the wonderful deeds of him who called you out of darkness into his marvelous light."

When I saw my ten-year-old nephew in South Carolina two weeks ago, this bright but physically frail little boy made what was for him a poignant revelation: "Uncle Kyle, when the boys play baseball, they never pick me." How sad it is to be excluded! But how vastly more tragic it is to be chosen and to exclude oneself. "The spirit itself bears witness with our spirits that we are the children of God, and if children, heirs, heirs of God and joint-heirs with Jesus Christ, if so be that we suffer with him that we may also be glorified together." Everything hangs on that "IF." God picks you for his purpose in this place, "that you may declare the wonderful deeds of him who called you out of darkness into his marvelous light." God is in the world seeking through his spirit and through his people the creation of free men in communion.

THE OPEN SECRET OF PENTECOST

by BEN M. HERBSTER

President, United Church of Christ

In the New Testament there are three words stemming directly out of, and motivated by, the Pentecost experience which the church needs to recapture. They become very evident as we read the Acts of the Apostles, particularly as we read that book at one sitting. I commend this discipline to you. Part of our difficulty is that usually we read the books of the Bible chapter by chapter, instead of book by book. Thus we see little or no connection between the various chapters and actually between the various books. Why not, before you continue to read this sermon, stop and read the Acts of the Apostles at one sitting? Then you will be ready to understand what follows.

The three words which I call to your attention are *witness, fellowship,* and *power.* The early church was a church of witness, of fellowship, and of power. Without these the church would have died aborning. With them, the church was more than sufficient to the task against which she was launched.

First of all, the church was a witnessing *fellowship.* The early churchmen thought that their main responsibility was to witness to the experience which was theirs. That is the purpose of a witness: to tell what he has seen, what he has experienced, what he has heard with his own ears. These early churchmen were possessed by a rich experience. They had been with the

Lord; they had been called by him, they had heeded that call and had walked with him. They had heard him teach. They had watched little children come to him, had seen old people hang upon his words, and had observed how those in the middle stream of life had been challenged by his ideas. They had observed the tide of opposition on the part of the scribes and the Pharisees rising until it reached ominous proportions. They had been with him in the garden when he was arrested. They had gone with him to Pilate's judgment hall. There they had heard him condemned to death. They had seen him scourged and beaten. They had walked with him on the way to the cross. On Golgotha they had seen him crucified between two thieves. They had been a part of the funeral cortege that ended in Joseph's new-hewn tomb. Then they had gone up into the upper room and had barred the door and were so afraid. As one of their number said later, "We had thought that this One should redeem Israel"; and now this One was dead. It is hard for us to imagine how truly their hopes had been dashed to the ground. One of our own poets has expressed it:

> He died!
> And with him perished all that men hold dear;
> Hope lay beside him in the sepulcher,
> Love grew corse cold, and all things beautiful beside
> Died when he died.[1]

And then they had seen the risen Christ! I wish it were possible for us really to understand the difference that this made in their living. The trouble is that when we observe Good Friday we know that on the third day Christ arose. It is really im-

---

[1] "Hope," *Quotable Poems,* comp., Thomas Curtis Clark and Esther A. Gillespie (New York: Willet, Clark and Colby, 1928), I, 249.

possible for us to imagine how life must have looked to those people who did not know of the coming resurrection, who thought that when Christ died he was dead and that was all. If we could really understand how life looked to them, then we would know why it was that afterwards every place they went, every word they spoke was a reflection of, and a witness to, the resurrection. "The Lord is risen, the Lord is risen indeed." Never could they forget that.

Never could they say a word that did not somehow include this message, "This Jesus, whom ye crucified, hath God raised up, whereof we are all witnesses." Or the way that Paul expressed it, "To this day I have had the help that comes from God, and so I stand here testifying both to small and great, and saying nothing but what the prophets and Moses said would come to pass: that the Christ must suffer, and that, by being the first to rise from the dead, he would proclaim light both to the people and to the Gentiles." How could these early churchmen keep quiet when they had had such a great experience, when for them tragedy had been turned into triumph, despair had been turned into victory, death had been turned to life?

It appears as Jesus said at another time, "I tell you, if these were silent, the very stones would cry out." So they witnessed, and as they witnessed change was effected in the life of the people and in the life of the world. In the Acts you read, "And fear came upon every soul; and many wonders and signs were done through the apostles. And all who believed were together and had all things in common; . . . And the Lord added to their number day by day those who were being saved."

As I look about the church today, its first weakness stems from the fact that we do not count as our primary responsibility that of *witnessing.* Perhaps we do not witness because this experience of seeing the risen Lord has not been personal for us.

It is more true as was true with Job, "I had heard of thee by the hearing of the ear." That is, many of us possess a secondhand religion. The risen Lord is not real to us nor is the ever-recurring miracle of what the risen Lord does for a man in whom he is. We have heard the message so often that it no longer stabs us wide-awake. We can read the words out of the Revelation, for instance, and be no more excited by them than if they were speaking of a sale that "Gimbels" is going to promote tomorrow.

Two things, therefore, are necessary if the church is to be the church. First of all, the people of the church have to have an experience with the risen Lord. His resurrection must become real. We must really believe that he died and rose again and lives forever more, and that because he lives we too shall live. These shall be not just words to us but truth, the living truth, the truth that transforms us so that we are never the same again; the truth that makes us literally new creations in Christ Jesus, our Lord.

In the second place, we must speak forth to what we have experienced. We must witness to this; about this we must tell, so that others shall have the self-same experience that has been ours. For Christ died and rose again not only for us but for all mankind. We must lose our reticence. We must become as men and women with one idea. "The Lord is risen, the Lord is risen indeed"; "and has committed unto us the word of reconciliation."

By and large we do not do this. We seem to be more reluctant to share our faith than anything else we have. If we have a new automobile, we gladly tell our neighbors about it. We brag about its superior points. We recommend this car to others. If we have a new kind of television, we invite all our neighbors to view a special program through its superior mechanism. We say, "You ought to have one too." But when it comes to our faith, we somehow operate on the supposition that faith is too personal a thing to talk about to others; that it matters not what you believe, just so you believe something; and if you believe nothing that matters little too.

The church must be a witnessing community. Unless we are that, we are nothing. This is the task to which we are called. This is the responsibility that is laid upon us. This is the job in which we must excel. If we fail here, we fail every place. "This Jesus, whom ye crucified, hath God raised up, whereof we are all witnesses." Are we? That is the question. Are we witnesses to the risen Lord?

But our Lord never for one moment discounted the proportions of the task to which he was calling his people. He knew the difficulty; he understood the problems they would confront; he knew it would not be easy; he understood the opposition, the hatred, the prejudice, the fears, the suspicions, the misunderstandings, the charges that would be leveled against them, and so he did not send his disciples out alone; he sent them out in company with their fellows.

He established his church so that the church could provide at once two kinds of help. It would be first of all a launching pad, if you please, for forays into the world. It would be a fellowship from which people went forth as such. The people who went forth could always know that the fellowship was behind them. I think you catch a little of the meaning of this if you read the thirteenth chapter of the Acts, beginning with the second verse, where the experience of the church at Antioch is recorded: "While they were worshiping the Lord and fasting, the Holy Spirit said, 'Set apart for me Barnabas and Saul for the work to which I have called them.' Then after fasting and praying they laid their hands on them and sent them off."

That is, as Paul and Barnabas went forth, they went forth as missionaries from the home church carrying with them the prayers and the concern and the encouragement and the strength of the home church. They did not count themselves alone. They knew the church went with them.

But there was another half of this, and that was that after Paul and Barnabas had been out in the world, had been beaten, and had become bruised and battered, they could return to the home church and there find a welcome and an understanding. There they could be refreshed and encouraged for the next foray into the world. Both of these aspects are most important. It is because we have forgotten part of this that the church is no stronger than she is.

We must understand anew that the church and the work of the church is not to be done in the church but in the world; that the church is a fellowship of people to send forth "task forces" into the world. The church was founded not for the sake of the church but for the sake of the world; for it is in the world that men live and die without Christ; it is in the world that men need what the Gospel can give to them; it is in the world that the Gospel of reconciliation must be proclaimed and lived. So the church must ever be a launching pad for its mission to the world.

This means that the whole stance of the church must be changed. We ministers sometimes say one of our hardest tasks is to find jobs for the members of the church to do; that if all of them would volunteer on any particular Sunday we would not know what to do with them. But you see this is because when we say "to find jobs for the members to do," we mean to find jobs for them to do *in* the church. There are just so many people that can sing in the choir and teach church school classes and be on committees and be members of the official board and do the ushering. Now I am not minimizing any of these tasks, for they all have to be accomplished. One of the difficulties is that usually we have a shortage of people even to do these.

But if one looks for jobs in which people can be engaged, if one looks for them not within the church but within the world, then there is no shortage of jobs, for the world at every point cries out for change, for transformation. Every place one looks there is a need that must be met, and the world is perishing for the need of just what the Gospel can provide. God is still saying, "Set apart for me Barnabas and Saul for the work to which I have called them."

But by the same token, the church must be a place to which, when people are fatigued, discouraged, disheartened, tired, battered, and bruised, they can return in order that there they may gather again their strength so that they can return to the world's tasks. There is a feeling that is possible only within the fellowship of the church; there is a refreshment a man cannot get in solitude; there is encouragement that comes only from the group which shares with him a faith in our Lord Jesus Christ and an experience of fellowship and oneness with him. In short, there must be within the church an alternation between going forth and coming back; between a launching pad and a home base. All this is what we mean when we talk about the fellowship of the church and this is the reason why the word and the idea, "fellowship," loom so large, both in the Acts of the Apostles and in the experience of the early church.

The third great word is *power*. It is as if God also knew that even with the encouragement and strength which comes from the fellowship we would be insufficient for the task to which he has called us, and so he promises us his *power*. We are to go forth not in our own strength but in his strength. The very basic marching orders included the promise of his power. "Go, therefore, and make disciples of all nations, baptizing them in the name of the Father and of the Son and of the Holy Spirit, teaching them to observe all that I have commanded you; and lo, I am with you always, even unto the end of the world."

This same promise is renewed by our Lord when on that day the disciples asked, "Lord, will you at this time restore the kingdom of Israel?" He said to them, "It is not for you to know times or seasons which the Father has fixed by his own authority. But you shall receive power when the Holy Spirit has come upon you; and you shall be my witnesses in Jerusalem and in all Judea and Samaria and to the end of the earth." And the glory is that this which he promised they found to be true and we still find it to be true.

Did you ever stop to think how few resources these disciples possessed that we would think were essential, if we were to go forth to launch a world-wide movement. They had no money, they had no education, they had no status, and they had no recognition. They had so little, but actually they had so much. So much, that sometimes we think it is so trivial and unimportant, that we spend no time getting it. They had the power of God and that was more than enough. "I will be with you always even unto the end of the world." In the light of that power they were more than sufficient.

The contrast between their fearfulness and their courage before and after Pentecost is nothing short of fantastic. In the upper room they barred the door, so fearful were they. But after Pentecost they went out and literally snapped their fingers under the nose of the Roman Empire, oblivious to all the chances they were taking, all the dangers they were encountering, all the difficulties they had to overcome. Their strength was not the strength of earth but of heaven. Paul himself cried out, "I can do all things in him who strengthens me." This was a tre-

92

mendous claim. Anyone who reads his life cannot help but know it was no exaggeration; he was able to do all things through Christ.

And this has been the long history of the church. Whenever the church has allowed itself to be filled with power, God's power, whenever the church has followed the disciplines of meditation, of prayer, of self-denial through which the power of God is available, then the church has been strong, much stronger than the world. Conversely, whenever the church has been timid, whenever the church has been more interested in gathering for herself status, position, wealth, then the church has been weak. The church cannot fulfill her mission without God's power and the church does not have to be without that power. This is the point: God is more ready and willing to give us of his power than we are to accept it.

Pentecost—Pentecostal witness, Pentecostal fellowship, Pentecostal power! This is what the early church knew and this is the reason why the early church grew as she grew. In two and one-half centuries, starting with nothing, the church became victor even over Rome and Constantine, and blazoned the cross upon the banner of the "Eternal City." Indeed it is an unbelievable saga that was written; an unbelievable chapter that was penned; an unbelievable life that was lived; but not so unbelievable that we cannot duplicate it in our days. But we cannot expect to duplicate it except by the self-same pattern they followed. *Witness, fellowship, power!* This is God's way, God's way for his church. Today, let us walk in that way and by his power accomplish his mission.

DIVINE FALL-OUT

by OSWALD HOFFMANN

Speaker, The Lutheran Hour, Lutheran Church—
Missouri Synod, St. Louis, Mo.

ACTS 2:38-39

The city is Jerusalem. The occasion: a national celebration.
Suddenly an explosion takes place—a blast so powerful that it
cannot be measured in megatons. The resultant fall-out blankets
every nation in the world, visibly altering the lives and destinies
of millions and millions of people.

What are we talking about? A hypothetical beginning of
World War III? The explosion of a great nuclear warhead?

We are talking about the celebration of a feast, a quite
ordinary feast made extraordinary by what happened that day.
It is Pentecost, marked by a great event: the coming of the Holy
Spirit to the followers of Jesus Christ.

The coming of the Spirit of God on that first Christian Pentecost was a super-nuclear explosion—the divine fall-out of
which has been descending upon the world for more than
1,900 years.

What kind of an explosion was it that produced such fall-
out?

Let's take a look at the count-down which preceded the
unleashing of this force, rocking the lives of people down

through the centuries. The explosion was planned. It did not come about by accident. The men who saw it happen were not exactly surprised. To them it was the end of a long train of events and the beginning of another.

Following our Lord for three years, constantly expecting him to unveil his kingly power, their hopes were crushed when he was seized and crucified. Down and out, they were stunned first by the news that he had risen from the dead and then by graphic demonstrations that he was really alive. For forty days he appeared to them at intervals, discussing with them the affairs of the Kingdom of God, and committing to them a charge to proclaim the gospel of the kingdom throughout all the world. Just before ascending into heaven, he instructed them to wait in the city of Jerusalem for fulfillment of a promise: "You shall receive power after the Holy Spirit has come upon you."

They waited, but they did not twiddle their thumbs. "With one accord, they all devoted themselves to prayer," searching for the meaning of his promise and waiting for it to be fulfilled.

Then it happened. They were all together. The world has never recovered from it.

Blast off minus ten was the ascension of Christ into heaven. Blast off minus fifty was his resurrection from the dead. Blast off minus fifty-three was his crucifixion on a hill outside the city wall. All this took place in accordance with divine plan, the preparations for which went into effect when a Baby was born in a little town south of Jerusalem.

Preparation had taken a long time. Peter recalled some of it to his audience on that first Pentecost: "This is that which was spoken by the prophet Joel: It shall come to pass in the last days, saith God, I will pour out my Spirit upon all flesh . . . it shall come to pass that whosoever shall call upon the name of the Lord shall be saved. Ye men of Israel, hear these words: Jesus of Nazareth, a Man approved of God among you by miracles and wonders and signs, which God did by him in the midst of you as ye yourselves also know; him, being delivered by the determinate counsel and foreknowledge of God, ye have taken, and by wicked hands have crucified and slain. Whom God hath raised up, having loosed the pains of death, because it was not possible that he should be holden of it . . . This Jesus hath God raised up, whereof we all are witnesses . . . having received of the Father the promise of the Holy Ghost, he hath shed forth this, which ye now see and hear. . . Therefore let all the house of Israel know assuredly that God hath made that same Jesus whom ye have crucified both Lord and Christ."

There it is. The count-down ended. The event took place. The divine fall-out began to descend. People asked what it all meant. They have been asking ever since.

What does it mean? It means that God is at work in the world through his Holy Spirit. Where does this fact put you and me? Right where those men were who wondered on that first Pentecost what they could do. Peter replied, "Repent and be baptized every one of you in the name of Jesus Christ for the remission of sins, and you shall receive the gift of the Holy Ghost, for the promise is unto you, and to your children, and to all that are afar off, even as many as the Lord our God shall call."

Peter and his associates staked their lives on the presence of the Holy Spirit of God. From that moment on, the tiny band of beaten, discouraged men, filled with terror and devoid of hope, was transformed into the growing multitude who through the ages, in spite of ridicule and contempt, have resolutely affirmed their faith in Christ the Savior. They are to be found today in every land, under every circumstance, their hearts filled with joy and their lives illuminated by hope. They are living evidence of the divine fall-out which has not lost its power, convincing witnesses to the presence of the Spirit as Christ promised: "You shall receive power when the Spirit comes upon you."

The explosion has taken place. The fall-out has been dropping ever since. The stirring pages of the book of Acts tell how it began to affect the lives of people. In unexpected ways, the old barriers and prejudices were broken down. New hope invaded the world. Bridges of love began to form. Outsiders remarked: "Behold, how they love one another." Others complained, "These men are turning the world upside down." When the divine fall-out penetrates a man's life, he can never be the same again.

Can it be true for us, living in a world where fall-out holds nothing but terror? Is it possible that the divine power can have any meaning for us, so far removed from that first Pentecost in this age of refrigerators and rockets? Is the Spirit of God really active in our time when so many churches are either tradition-choked, or as J. B. Phillips has put it, "enjoying fascinating sidetracks"? Where is the transforming power of God's Holy Spirit?

The Danish philosopher Kierkegaard described the all too common situation in the form of a parable. There was a flock of geese in the farmyard. Once each week the geese would waddle from their pens to the barn where they would sing hymns and listen to a leader goose speak to them about the geese of years gone by. One time, he told them, the same kind of geese as they were, with the very same kind of wings, used to fly into the sky. The geese were stirred by these words and after singing another hymn, waddled back to their pens until the next week when they would again hear how geese used to flap the same kind of wings they had and fly into the sky.

The point of the parable, of course, is that Christians of today often are satisfied with memories of the past, but fail to act in the present with the courage of faith. Empty words are no substitute for the life-giving power of the Holy Spirit.

The life-giving power of the Spirit is present in God's living Word. "The promise is unto you," Peter declared. The Word must come from God to kindle the flame of faith. Coming from God, the Good News of Christ the Savior is borne along on wings of the Spirit to stir the hearts of men, convicting them of sin and convincing them of their Savior. Where is the power of the Spirit? It is there wherever the Savior is proclaimed, wherever the Word of God is preached, wherever men witness to their faith in Christ with lips and life.

The fall-out of God's Word upon the world, with all the blessings it brings, can be turned aside by the leaden shelters men build against it. These are the shelters of pride and self-will, of resolute refusal to listen to God and willful determination to go every way except God's way. Those shelters are tombs.

"Repent," said St. Peter, "and be baptized every one of you in the name of Jesus Christ for the remission of sins, and ye shall receive the gift of the Holy Ghost." There is an urgency in this appeal. It is a matter of life and death as Christ himself emphasized: "Unless you are born anew of water and the Spirit, you will never enter the kingdom of God." Break out of your shell, present yourself before God, repent, and be baptized for the remission of sins. This is the appeal of the gospel, coming with the power of God's Holy Spirit.

Repent! Turn away from your sin—your bickering, your self-pity, and self-will. Turn away from your pride, that self-right-eousness which makes you trust in yourself. Repent and be baptized in the name of Jesus Christ, every one for the forgiveness of your sins!

Christ is the source and Christ is the center of the Spirit-filled Word of God. He was crucified for the forgiveness of our sins. There is no gospel except the Good News of the forgiveness of sins in the name of Jesus Christ. If you have not been baptized in the name of Christ, the words of Peter are unmistakably clear: "Repent and be baptized." If you have been baptized and have forgotten what it means to be a disciple of Christ, repent and take new hold of the Savior in whose name you were baptized and by whom you are forgiven.

Ordinary people who believe in Christ can be the temple of the Holy Spirit, showing forth the power and the glory of God in their ordinary lives. Do not look to your own feelings. Look to Christ your Savior. Hold onto him. Accept the assurance of the Spirit that, baptized in the name of Jesus Christ, you are really forgiven; by faith you are a child of God, on your way to God.

Don't be discouraged by the fact that the church today does not always display the same vitality which was evident in the early church. You can't get along without the church. Don't draw the conclusion that the Spirit is not present just because you don't notice his presence in the lives of some professing Christians round about you. The Spirit comes through the lowly tools of the gospel and the sacraments. He makes his presence known in people whose lives are nourished by the gospel and the sacraments. The Spirit is mightily at work today in unspectacular and unimpressive ways, but powerfully at work nonetheless. Remember, God's call is not to criticize others, but to repent and believe, to be baptized and forgiven.

Let the divine fall-out of the Spirit of God drop upon you. It will do for you what it did for the faithful followers of our Lord. In the fellowship of faith they were freed from the petty jealousies, the unfriendly cliques, and the rivalry for first seats which had characterized their own earlier relationships. Turning to the Lord in continuous prayer and supplication, they waited for the fulfillment of the Lord's promise. Filled with the Holy Spirit, they went forth to proclaim the Word of God with power.

Don't wait. The big explosion has occurred, the fall-out is coming down. Christ has died for your sins. The Spirit is knocking at your door with the promise of forgiveness in the name of Christ. Don't wait. The promise is to you and to your children. Repent and be baptized in the name of Jesus Christ for the forgiveness of your sins. The gift, my friend, of the Spirit is yours. Amen.

BRETHREN, WHAT SHALL WE DO?

by GERALD KENNEDY

Bishop, Los Angeles Area, The Methodist Church

"And Peter said to them, 'Repent, and be baptized everyone of you in the name of Jesus Christ for the forgiveness of your sins; and you shall receive the gift of the Holy Spirit. For the promise is to you and to your children and to all that are far off, everyone whom the Lord our God calls to him.' "

—ACTS 2:38-39

When Peter preached at Pentecost, his audience did not say at the close of the sermon that it was eloquent or that they enjoyed it. They asked what they could do. There is no surer sign of great preaching than such a response. If Peter had been one of the non-directive fellows, he might have asked them what they had in mind. Instead, he gave them a direct answer and his words form the outline of what I want to say today.

The setting, of course, is Pentecost which was the beginning of the Christian church and, in my judgment, one of the great events in all history. The disciples had been through the harrowing and tragic events of Holy Week and then they had seen and heard the witness of the resurrection. They had no immediate idea of what they ought to do. They were waiting in

Jerusalem, as the Scripture says, "in one place." Suddenly the great event happened, and they found it impossible to describe except in terms of poetry. It was the sound of a mighty wind; the appearance of tongues of fire.

They did not receive minute instructions for the rest of their lives but they did receive light upon the next step of their path. They knew they had to witness and they went out into the streets, being given the gift of speaking the language of the various tribes and nations. Some of the people accused them of being drunk. In answer to that charge Peter stood up and preached his great sermon, going back to the beginning of biblical history and proclaiming that the coming of Jesus was the fulfillment of a promise God had made through the Scriptures. So, being convicted in their hearts with the need for a response to the message, Peter told them they must repent, they must be baptized, they must receive the gift of the Holy Spirit, and that this was for them and for their children and for those near and those afar off.

Let us look first at his demand that they must

Repent.

This is a harsh, hard word, and to modern ears it sounds old-fashioned. It means to change the direction we are going and to reorganize our lives. It means to find new values to live by and to confess that we have taken the wrong turning. The word does not fit our modern vocabulary and it does not agree with our modern ideas.

The church needs this word because it is obvious that there is something deeply wrong with us. In some ways everything looks fine for we have numbers and we have valuable properties.

We are quite willing to launch a new crusade or establish a new program but to be told that the need is for a deep and abiding re-evaluation of our life is not heard gladly. We would much rather tinker with our machinery and establish a few new committees.

The command that we should repent is not received gladly by persons. We want happiness all right, but we do not intend to pay any big price for it. We still believe that there is some secret that can be discovered so that without very much bother, we may have joy and find meaning again for our living. It is as if we were saying of the old car that a new coat of paint will do it in spite of the fact that the motor is obviously inadequate.

Repentance means to take a long look backward and find where we went wrong. It means to confess that once we knew something we no longer know and that once we had an experience which we have lost. It means saying that we are wrong and we cannot blame it on circumstances or other people. It means also to take a forward look and dare to give our allegiance to a new master. It means we must establish a new routine as a pattern of our living. Indeed, the Fourth Gospel puts it so radically that it shocks us as it did Nicodemus. It says that we must be born again and that the change in our lives must be as complete as receiving a new birth.

There was once a traveler who stopped to ask a man by the side of the road how far it was to his destination. "Well," said the man, "if you keep on going the way you are going it is about 25,000 miles. But if you will turn back and take a right turn, it is about three miles." This was the word Peter spoke to those men and it is a word for us. To keep on going the way we are going means that we will never arrive where we want to be.

The second thing that Peter said was

Be Baptized.

I do not intend to go into any long discussion of the meaning of baptism nor to debate one form against another. I do not desire to enter into any argument over infant baptism as opposed to adult baptism. My own church does both and uses the form desired by the person to be baptized. We regard it as a sacrament and as a sign of entrance into a new fellowship and a new life. It is the commitment of a person to the church and to the Kingdom.

Now I can imagine that this was a hard word for those people. They might have said that while they felt a need for what Peter had been preaching, they did not want to associate themselves with the scum of the earth. For even St. Paul had to admit that there were not many great, not many rich, and not many wise, who were members of those early churches. There was not a key person in the community who belonged. Many a man must have felt that to join this group was to lower his social status beyond any reasonable level. Becoming a part of the disinherited was too big a price to pay for the salvation Peter had promised in his sermon.

We are not free from this feeling today. Indeed, the trend among some young preachers to put their emphasis on quality instead of quantity may very well be the ancient gnostic heresy. No one should object to emphasizing full commitment from church members. But to suggest that the church is for a few who are going to go deep into the meaning of religion and not for the many who may never be able to go that deep, is a heresy the church has fought against from the beginning. It is very difficult for people to believe that the church ought to be open

104

to every man on the level that he is capable of understanding and achieving.

I was pastor of a church one time in a university community. There were a number of professors who were members and some of them were Ph.D's. They formed a little group which they wanted me to attend and although I resisted as long as possible, finally I could find no more excuses and began to meet with them. They wanted to study books which the ordinary member of the congregation could not understand and they were self-consciously aware that they could go deeper than others. I stayed with them for a while and then I left them for it came to me that I was pastor of the whole church and not of an aristocratic minority. We are on the wrong track when we talk about quality versus quantity in a Christian church for we ought to have both.

When a man commits himself to this fellowship, he is saying as Martin Luther said a long time ago, "Here I stand." He becomes a part of the men and women and young people who have banded together to become followers of Jesus Christ. He is saying to the world that he believes what the church stands for and that this faith is transmitted and preserved by the Christian church. He is saying that he is willing to walk with these people, great and small, rich and poor, young and old, intellectual and ignorant. The older I grow the more willing I am to proclaim to all the world without apology that I am a member of the Christian church.

A man said to his pastor one day that he had had an experience the night before which he thought could be made into a sermon. He was coming home from a shipyards late at night in a Scotland town. His pay was in his pocket and he was very nervous when he heard footsteps following him in the dark street. He speeded up but they speeded up also, and when he slowed up, they seemed to slow up to the same pace. Finally, he came to the stairs that led up to the next street and he rushed up them and at the top, turned and said in a kind of desperation, "What do you want? Who are you?" A little girl came out of the shadows and told him that she had stayed too late at her grandmother's and was trying to find her way home in the darkness. She was frightened and thought that maybe she could follow him and he would help her. The man told his pastor how he had taken her by the hand and had led her home. Ah indeed, that is the church which surrounds us with care and concern and points us in the direction we must go.

The third thing that Peter said at the close of his sermon was that they must

Receive the Holy Spirit.

I can imagine those men saying that it was about time the preacher offered them something instead of demanding something from them. Surely, there must be a premium to receive, surely there must be a prize to be won. Here it is at last and they grasp this promise with satisfaction.

We have become what might be called a trading stamp generation. Of course, ultimately we pay for the trading stamps and the prizes but it makes us feel good to think that if we buy a product, we get something extra free. I remember some time ago traveling in Arizona with a man who was saving a certain kind of trading stamp which could be obtained at certain gasoline stations. I sat on the edge of the seat many a time because I was worried that we would run out of gas in 110 degree temperature. But he would not make a purchase until he found the station which gave the stamps.

All our commercials, especially on television, promise us

something extra if we buy. Are you not amazed at the number of deodorants which are being promoted today? What an ill-smelling generation we must be according to the commercials. Ah, but in addition to smelling good, we will get romance if we buy this particular product. Or you may buy a can of beer and achieve relaxation and peace of mind. You do not have to read the books by the popular preachers but simply buy a can of beer and get all of this ease. Dog foods are provided in all shapes and qualities and if you get the right one, you will get the love of your dog which is a whole lot better than no love at all. The used car pitchmen will give you transportation that is cheaper than walking and give you status in your community.

Just as we are settling down to enjoy the premium, we begin to think about this phrase "the Holy Spirit." Wait a minute! Is this not the Spirit of God? Yes, it is. But can any man see God and live? And what will happen to a man if the Spirit of God possesses him? Will we too feel sensitivity to pain and have a sense of the suffering of the world? Will we be more aware of the needs of our brethren and their claims upon us? Yes, I am afraid we will.

Does the Spirit of God bring courage? Yes, it does. But courage is what gets us into trouble. Courage makes a man stand up and speak a word when he would be unnoticed if he kept quiet. Courage drives a man to stand with a minority and go contrary to the customs of his time. It is much more comfortable to find out which way the wind blows and trim our sails accordingly.

Is there any joy connected with the Holy Spirit? Yes, there is. But there was a book called Hebrews written by someone whose name we do not know who said that Jesus endured the cross for the joy that was set before him. Is this the kind of joy

107

the Holy Spirit will bring upon us? It may very well be. We are not sure that we are willing to receive this kind of joy.

There was a young Presbyterian minister who was having a very happy pastorate. Some of the old ministers in his presbytery were sure that he could not be preaching orthodoxy and producing so much joy among the people. They formed a committee to examine his theology. He answered all the enquiries gladly and easily. Finally the chairman of the committee asked the question which he had seen saving, "Are you willing," he asked, "to be damned for the glory of God?" "Yes," replied the young minister, "I am; and not only that but I am willing for this whole presbytery to be damned for the glory of God." And so we have a feeling that the Holy Spirit will carry us further than we are willing to go. There is nothing safe in it. We draw back in fear and yet, deep in our hearts, there is an assurance that if we were what we ought to be, we would be filled with the Spirit of God. Finally, it comes to us that this is what we have been seeking all our lives and this alone is what gives our living meaning and purpose. Out of our repentance and out of our commitment to the church there comes joy of the Holy Spirit.

Finally, St. Peter's word is that this experience is for

Everyone.

It is for those of one generation and for all the generations. It is to those who are afar off twenty centuries in the future. It is to us and today we dare believe that it is for those who are in the future and far beyond us. Here is something universal and eternal and absolute. Here is the thing which is for every man and every age.

During the last century or so, Protestants have tended to
108

stress their differences and more than 250 denominations in the United States indicate how easy it is to divide on the basis of opinions. There are a number of denominations whose birth was out of bitterness and controversy. In our seeking for orthodoxy we have often sacrificed love.

It is a joy to all of us that the trend is now reversed and instead of dividing we seem to be coming together again. How wonderful it is to know that there is so much more to unite us than there is to separate us. We all have a common faith which rests upon certain great affirmations to which we all subscribe. We all have a common need whether we are young or old, rich or poor, black or white. We all have a common Lord to whom we have pledged our allegiance, whom we have promised to follow wherever he leads us. We believe that our Lord is the one who will reform the world and redeem our society.

Yet as we come together with our common need and our common faith and our common discipleship, we discover this does not rob us of our individuality but rather it increases our sense of importance as persons. For we hear a voice which was described by the prophet Isaiah saying, "Fear not, for I have redeemed you; I have called you by name, you are mine." So as we belong together, we come to see that we are not simply a statistic in a survey, or a vote in an election, or a purchaser in an economic system. We are rather the ones for whom Christ died and we are rescued out of our anonymity into a new sense of our dignity, our importance, and our high calling. He calls us together when he redeems our separate souls and restores us to the status of persons called to be his sons and daughters.

Some years ago there was a circus fire at Hartford, Connecticut, and a number of people burned to death. Among them was a little girl whose name was unknown and they waited for someone to claim her but no one did. Finally, she was buried in a little coffin with just the number 1565 on it. Someone whose name we do not know wrote a poem and the closing lines are these:

> There she lies as no one still,
> Nameless on a lonely hill,
> And the snowflakes and the rain
> Come and go and fall again
> On little Miss Nobody.

Those of us who have lost our way find ourselves mere members of a crowd listening anxiously for a word of identification. Who are we anyway? Then Pentecost comes again and the preaching of the apostle redeems each of us who are nobodies. We follow his commands and from our isolation we are restored to fellowship. Then we become somebody, indeed!

PENTECOST AND THE DIVIDED WORLD

by DAISUKE KITAGAWA

Executive Secretary, Division of Domestic
Mission, National Council of the Protestant
Episcopal Church of the U. S. A.; Former
Secretary, Secretariat of Racial and Ethnic
Relations, World Council of Churches

"While . . . they were all together in one place
. . . . There appeared to them tongues like
flames of fire, dispersed among them and resting
on each one. And they were filled with the Holy
Spirit and began to talk in other tongues. . . ."

—ACTS 2:2-4 (NEB)

Today we are living in a world which is at once united and
divided. Science and technology have all but conquered geo-
graphical distance and we no longer think of the world in
terms of "five continents and seven seas." Far from the "new
heaven and the new earth" though we are, in this world of ours
there is a sense in which the "sea is no more" (Rev. 21:1) in
that the entire world has virtually become a neighborhood—one
global society. The dream of Cecil Rhodes, the colonial im-
perialist *par excellence* of the nineteenth century, is not very far
from being realized: "What a pity that we cannot get to the

111

stars, shining overhead at night . . . I'm sorry to see them so clear and at the same time so far."[1] Now the moon has been reached and has become our next door neighbor in this space age!

By the same token, increasing numbers of cities, wherever they may be located, are becoming truly international in their population makeup—microcosms. "Now there were living in Jerusalem devout Jews drawn from every nation under heaven" (Acts 2:5, NEB). Similarly, in Geneva, in Paris, in New York, in London, in Tokyo, in Hong Kong, people "from every nation under heaven" are found, visiting, residing, trading, studying, and associating one with another. And it is not only in those metropolitan centers that the population is cosmopolitan, but increasing numbers of much smaller cities are growing just as much so.

Especially, when one thinks not only in terms of people but of all the factors that make up one's own life—the foods one eats, the books one reads, the music one enjoys, the clothes one wears—all of which together enrich one's life to be what it is—it may not be too much of an exaggeration to say that every town, village, and hamlet, no matter where on earth, is now a microcosm!

As man conquers distance and makes a neighborhood of the whole world, the world in its entirety comes into man's life. The habitat of modern man is no less than the whole world, and the whole world lives within modern man as his "internal environment." Thus, today, we live in *one* world indivisible.

At the same time, no one can deny that ours is also a divided and fragmented world. Oceans may no longer divide mankind, but "curtains" of various kinds do constitute invincible "walls

[1] Quoted by Dr. Nikolai Federenko in his paper, "The Soviet Union and African Countries," in the *Annals of The American Academy of Political and Social Science, CCCLIV* (July, 1964), p. 2.

of partition," among which the ideological and the racial are deemed to be of the most serious kind. These walls do not keep one nation apart from another but turn every nation into a "house divided against itself."

Equally serious is the divisive tendency inherent in specialization, both academic and professional. Intelligent and responsible citizens who belong to one and the same local community, be it a university or a municipality, can be hopelessly divided by the technical jargons they, as specialists, are compelled to use in order to be at their professional or academic best. Herein is a phenomenon that may aptly be called a "modern tower of Babel," the confusion of languages! This in turn divides each person's life inwardly into professional life, family life, and civic life. Modern man living in such a divided world is likely, then, to become a split personality.

The basic problem of modern man lies in the fact that he is destined to live in a world in which both *unitive* and *divisive* forces are at work simultaneously. His problem lies in that, on the horns of the dilemma, he cannot choose either one or the other, but he has to live with both. It is a world as much built by man as created by God! Indeed, man has been destined, ever since the Fall, to be a builder of the city, a civilization. "Cain knew his wife, and she conceived and bore Enoch; and he built a city, and called the name of the city after the name of his son, Enoch" (Gen. 4:17).

The world in which we live and which lives in us is a world essentially urban in its character. It is not a naturally grown thing like the primitive village, but built under God by man, like the modern city. Man, the city-builder is not he who was in the primeval state of innocence in the Garden of Eden but he who has "eaten of the tree of knowledge" and who has become conscious of his identity as man and has since been on the pilgrimage toward "the Promised Land," the new Jerusalem. Called by God to be a free moral agent within the limit of his creatural finiteness, man is to fulfill his manhood through his unconditional obedience to God in unrestrained freedom of his will. Or, it may be said that only unrestrained freedom under unconditional obedience to God will ultimately bring man to the new Jerusalem.

In the meantime man within history can have neither unrestrained freedom (because of his creatural finiteness) nor unconditional obedience to God (due to the sinfulness of his nature) and every creative effort made by him with the best of intentions and the purest of motives is marred by some destructive elements. "Come, let us build ourselves a city, and a tower with its top in the heavens" (Gen. 11:4) and this tower was to be built with the brick made by their own hands!

Before they made much progress, however, these men were scattered because in the course of this noble enterprise their languages were confused and they ceased to understand one another (Gen. 11:7-8). Thus the original unity of mankind in its primeval state of undifferentiated wholeness (Gen. 11:1) was lost forever, and ever since mankind has been seeking to be reintegrated so as to regain its wholeness—not by looking backward to the lost paradise but forward to the promised land.

It is no less than this pilgrimage that modern man is engaged in through his effort to build a one-world society with all the ingenuity he can muster, which in the beginning God imparted in him.

Philosophy and science, technology and engineering are all means by which man under God, that is, in his God-given freedom, is to fulfill that potentiality which God in the beginning imparted in him. Man's creatural finiteness, however, makes it impossible for man to see everything more than *partially* like "puzzling reflections in a mirror" (1 Cor. 13:12, NEB). Herein is the inevitable necessity for specialization, without which there could not have been such progress in various branches of science, and consequently the one-world society we now are living in.

And, be it noted, it is precisely through the very same specialization that our world is becoming a house which is internally divided, in which specialists know more and more about less and less, and the ordinary run of people know less and less about more and more, and between them very little communication. The "Tower of Babel" all over again.

Yet, we are not to look back to that state of "dreamy innocence," to borrow Professor Tillich's phrase,[2] or the time when "the whole earth had one language and few words" (Gen. 11:1). We are to look forward to the promised land, the new Jerusalem, the heavenly city, built "at unity in itself" (Ps. 122:3, *Book of Common Prayer*).

That is to say, we are not to reject specialization but to go beyond specialization. Specialization without co-ordination will inevitably bring about confusion, at however high a level it might be! Specialization is essential to technical expertise. Essential to co-ordination are, on one hand, humility and openness—what the Bible calls "meekness": "the meek shall inherit the earth"—and, on the other hand, the will to relate one's self to others—what the Bible calls "love," which is the highest gift of the Holy Spirit.

Even in the primitive church in Corinth, there were *specialists* of various kinds who were serving God through their specialized skills, which at the same time, one suspects, caused *division* within the church. In the face of this situation Paul's

[2] Paul Tillich, *Systematic Theology* (Chicago: University of Chicago, 1957) II, 33.

admonition to the church in Corinth was that all these different skills were gifts of the same Spirit, and the highest of all the gifts of the Spirit is that which unites all these skills so as to make them serve the total need of total man.

One may have all sorts of unusual talents or specialized skills, but without love such skills are more likely to separate one from other people, making one's knowledge profound but partial. With all the academic brilliance and professional expertise, a specialist who is unable to relate himself to others may contribute more to the confusion than to the reintegration of the world. Only when, with the aid and guidance of the Holy Spirit, the profoundest of the insights gained by specialists in one discipline are communicated to specialists of hosts of other disciplines, will a world be built which will be at unity with itself.

Herein is one dimension of the ministry of reconciliation committed to the church of Jesus Christ, within the context of the emerging one global society of mankind. Made up of men and women of all races, cultures, and professional disciplines, the church can be a living community of those who are deeply concerned about the ultimate destiny of mankind, in which specialists in every field may engage one another in an open conversation on a sustaining basis, each remaining at his professional best and yet finding ways to communicate one to another. They will be able to do this because the Holy Spirit will aid each of them to see his own specialization *in perspective* preventing him from idolizing or absolutizing his own contribution and motivating him humbly to learn from others so that they together in "faith, hope, and love" may see the whole truth. To this end, then, the church must pray that she may achieve her own unity; that is, for the purpose of becoming an effective instrument for the service of reintegrating the now divided world and in Christ reconciling it to God.

116

CHICAGO AND THE GATHERING OF THE NATIONS

by FRANKLIN H. LITTELL

Chicago Theological Seminary, Chicago, Ill.

The Christian movement began with a dramatic act of God, when the Spirit descended with power and the tiny colony of heaven was turned outward to grow and to fill the earth as the stars fill the heavens. By the Spirit the band of faithful few received power, that they should be a witnessing people—"in Jerusalem and in all Judea and Samaria and to the end of the earth" (Acts 1:8). At Pentecost, the Christians were grafted onto the work of Christ with power; even the sweet fellowship of those who had known Jesus in the flesh was no end in itself! They, and all who bear the Name after them, were reminded that the Christians are not here to please themselves, but that Christ's creation may be brought to fulfillment.

At every true ingathering, at every service of Commitment, we are reminded that in joining the Christian movement we have been recruited into the greatest march in history: the Exodus from civilizations—the exodus from violence and dehumanization, exploitation and racial strife, the hatreds and lusts and cruelties of the unbaptized world of the past. And the march of this New People ends only in the Kingdom of God, in the world as God intended it when he made all nations of one blood, in the order he purposed before men went over into rebellion against him. The Lord of the Christians, beloved, is no little household god, concerned only for private religion, in the individual and in the family. He is the God of the nations, though they know it not. He is the God of the heavens, before whom the peoples rise and fall. He is the creator, without whom all building is in vain, without whom "was not anything made that was made" (John 1:3). His purpose is justice and witness and peace. *This* is the line of march you have joined, and the direction and the end of it are sure. For this Exodus from the hostilities and anxieties of the uncertain past he is calling New Men and New Women to become fit citizens for the New World.

The first miracle of Pentecost is that they understood each other. Far back on the gray plains of our antiquity there stands a grim tower, monument to human pride and confusion. Babel, the tower of arrogance, ended in scattering and the end of building up and the confusion of the language of all the earth (Gen. 11:1-9). But the Babel of suspicion and animosity and hatred has been overcome in Pentecost, and now we hear them telling in their own tongues the mighty works of God (Acts 2:4); that which was broken and alienated by man's pride of race and station—our selfishness, our racism, our lust for power over others—has been sentenced to death by the mighty intervention of God the Spirit, and we begin to understand each other again.

How easily have we fallen into sin! How readily we accept the wickedness of corrupt land contracts, drawn to grind the faces of the poor! How instinctively we turn our hands to walls and towers to drive our unwanted neighbor back into his ghetto —forgetting that in the same moment we have left the line of

118

march of the holy nation, the people of royal priesthood, and embraced thereby again the confusions of heathenism! How often the peace of God is disturbed by hateful monologists, by those who broadcast to us from a sound proofed room, who shout aloud from the isolation of their sin and anxiety, but will not hear their brothers! At Pentecost men both listened and spoke, and God overcame their babble with the power of his healing and uniting Spirit.

To understand truly is to live someone else's experience as my own. Inspired by the recklessness of creative love, the faithful are attending the School of Christ—there to learn to practice "unlimited liability" for each other and for all his creatures. To love truly, as Martin Luther put it, is to "put on one's neighbor." I can abuse my neighbor by segregation, I can exploit him by sinful discrimination at school or on the job or in housing: that is, I can leave the line of march and again take the primrose bypaths to death and destruction. But then the prophet's judgment falls upon me (Is. 47:10-11). As long as we remain soldiers of the cross, we are in training for another life, another city: "the city which has foundations, whose builder and maker is God" (Hebr. 11:10). In this blessed city, for which citizenship we now have our first papers, I shall love my neighbor as myself.

The second miracle is that they come from many peoples and tribes. Chicago is a place like that, a gathering place of the nations. How many different cultures and peoples have gone into the making of this giant hog dealer, stock broker, corn merchant and of the world! Here in the heartland of America, in the city of Dwight L. Moody and Jane Addams and Carl Sandburg, we have one of the greatest power centers in the

119

history of mankind. Colleges and universities abound. There are more Protestant seminaries here than in any other city in the world, and we have a great work developing too in mission to the Inner City and in ecumenics—in interchurch co-operation where it counts. Here too is the greatest Roman Catholic archdiocese. Within a few years we shall have the greatest area where Negroes and whites live together in a single city of the globe. What kind of a city will it be? Suffering wasteland of confusion of tongues, or a base camp on the line of march toward the City of God?

At Pentecost each people is respected in its own integrity. In anticipation of the time when all shall be as one, each speaks his own questions and concerns and convictions—and is heard. The hatred of the Jew by the Gentiles in Hitler's Third Reich (and elsewhere, among heathen), as many students of totalitarian ideology have pointed out, was precisely because of his Jewishness. The hatred of the racists for the Negro, as a famous Negro writer has recently pointed out, is precisely because he doesn't look and act like a white man. But among those visited by the Spirit, another law and another order takes effect. The Christians look to the day when men of all races and tongues and colors shall be gathered about the hill of the Lord, and hear his law and obey his will. And in this vision of the universal Kingdom there is no place for the pride of life and natural place which affronts even the Least Brother.

The shame, the infamy of the twentieth century is precisely that in these bloody years so many so-called Christians have betrayed their Lord and reverted to old tribal religions. This is the religious challenge of Nazism, of the new "Great Russia"

imperialism, of Afrikaner *apartheid,* of the White Citizens
Councils and their allies in the spiritual underworld of America.
Tens of millions of the baptized have betrayed their baptism,
and without that betrayal the reproach of Nazism and Russian
Communism and American-style racism had never lain on
Christendom. The cause which you have joined is, if you mean
what you have said, a strenuous one. You have abandoned many
of the false and familiar idols by which men naturally set such
great store. But you will still have many attractive opportunities
to betray the Name which has been branded on your soul. On
the other hand you may, if you hold to the line of march, be
called upon to face the affrontery and arrogance of those who
still serve the princes and powers of this world's darkness—to
suffer, as the apostle wrote, to become as the filth and offscour-
ing of the world, to the glory of Christ (I Cor. 4:13-15). For
the dying world hates the cross of Christ, and fights as best it
can against the growing army of those who know that the judgment of God has already been passed upon it, and that a New
World is called into being, of which we are citizens-in-an-
ticipation.

None of us is called upon to imitate another or bow to
another because of his color or tongue or origin, or any other
marks of his being a creature. For *all* of us are called upon
to cast aside every weight and every burden and to become the
persons that he intended us to be when he created us, before
we took up arms in rebellion.

The third miracle of Pentecost is the visitation of power of
the Spirit, of the power of the age to come. For just as there
is a world—or an age—that is dying, so there is an age—a king-

121

dom—being born in us. By the fire and the rushing wind and the tongues we are instructed that no purely internal and private matter is involved.

". . . you shall receive power when the Holy Spirit has come upon you; and you shall be my witnesses in Jerusalem and in all Judea and Samaria and to the end of the earth" (Acts 1:8).

This is the promise.

"This Jesus God raised up and of that we all are witnesses" (Acts 2:32).

This is the reality, confirmed by the Spirit and attested by the apostles just before they turned to share with each according to his need. The interlocking relationships of these lessons is most significant. There is no living promise apart from service to one's neighbor. There is no power of the Spirit apart from response to the needs of the world, the world for which Christ died. We are empowered—not to personal retreat but to spiritual battle.

It is the Lordship of Jesus Christ over all of life which we proclaim.

"We repudiate the false teaching that there are areas of our life in which we belong not to Jesus Christ but another Lord, areas in which we do not need justification and sanctification through him" (Synod of Barmen, 1934).

What does this mean when translated into the concerns and decisions of everyday life? For it is on the job, where his

122

treasure is, that a man is known, and not primarily by his use of the "church language," the special dialect of Sunday mornings. Does he understand how he has been made a steward of talents, of gifts, in performing some perhaps highly specialized but very essential role in the great city of our time? If he is a policeman, his is the stewardship of law and order against anarchy and the jungle. If he is a teacher, his is a stewardship of the minds and spirits of children and youth—of the transmission of wisdom and culture across generations. If he is a doctor, his is the stewardship of the public health. If he works in personnel, his is the stewardship of personal relations at the moment of induction into some phase of the world's work. If any of these, or any of us in other roles in society, forget our calling and our stewardship and go over to the opposition—as if the policeman were to join the beasts of prey or the doctor to put greed for the dollar ahead of service to persons—then too we have betrayed the Name.

The basic fact about the emerging city is this: that community is no longer based primarily on the blood relationship of nomadic bands and wandering tribes. Neither is it based on neighborhoods, as though the city were an agglomeration of villages. This was the pattern of rural life, from which indeed many of us came. Community in the Great City is primarily vocational and professional, based on the sense of identity felt by those who share a common style of life and a "we-feeling" based on their place in the world's work. It is in the on-the-job relationships that we are tested: How transparently do our words and our decisions commend the universal church and her Lord to those with whom we live and work?

We are called to service and to a ministry. Every believing

Christian is, by virtue of the ordination of his baptism, a member of the ministry of the whole people of God. Those whom we generally call "ministers," that is, the clergy, are in fact best understood as chaplains to the *laos* in their work in the world. You new members, especially, are recruited to the general ministry. Volunteer service in the church is a worthy act, and many of you will grow into a fit place in the works, the organizational life of the institution. But it is service in the world which will bring scars and nobility, if worthily carried. After all, as a great Christian martyr, Dietrich Bonhoeffer, reminded us just a few years ago, Christ did not die for the church: he died for the *world*.

There are two cities here in Chicago, and two kinds of citizens. There is the city of those who believe that everything will stay—and must stay—just the way it is. They tell us that men will never change, that there will always be wars and racial strife and the law of the jungle in economic life. Their gospel is not the Good News that Christians know, that everything is being made new, but the bad news that everything must stay as it is. And then there is the city of those who have glimpsed, above the slums and the disease and the dirt and the clashing arms, the alabaster towers of shining brotherhood. You are called to be citizens of that second city, which will grow and grow until its fullness fills the earth with justice and righteousness and peace.

The Lord of that second city, the city which is superseding and replacing the old city of the past, is one whose name is Love: "His nature and His name is Love." That is the Truth, the Word, the pitch which was laid from the foundations of the world. That is the note by which all the morning stars sing together, and all the worlds that abide are made.

In the line of march, the people hear a music. They have joy, and a song. The dying world is tone-deaf, but the Christians have caught the pitch. And the pitch is given by Love Incarnate. In the words of the old spiritual,

> You just touch one string,
> And the whole heavens ring . . .

And the string that you touch is Love. AMEN.

PENTECOST'S CENTRIPETAL
AND CENTRIFUGAL POWER

Associate Professor of Church History, Divinity
School, University of Chicago; Associate Editor,
The *Christian Century*

ACTS 2 (NEB):

"While the day of Pentecost was running its course they were
all together in one place, when suddenly . . ." (vs. 1)

"We hear them telling in our own tongues the great things
God has done . . ." (vs. 11)

"For the promise is to you, and to your children, and to all who
are far away . . ." (vs. 39)

"They met constantly to hear the apostles teach, and to share
the common life . . ." (vs. 42)

Be clear on this: there are things that man cannot do. He cannot create "a new Pentecost." He cannot be the maker or the
re-maker of the church. He cannot create Christian unity. Pentecost was and is the movement of God the Holy Spirit to man.
The church is the gift of Jesus Christ to man. Christian unity

is the promise of the Father to his divided children. Be clear on this: there are things that man cannot do.

Why should we so stress the idea of man's inability to perform basic actions such as these? Is it for the sake of theological precision? Do we accent this so that we can once again satisfy ourselves that we have "checked in" at the first and cardinal doctrine of Christianity: that God is and acts and that we are creatures dependent on his action? Is it for the sake of finesse and neatness in defining a doctrine of man? They are important concerns, all of them. But our real reason for making clear the weakness of man in matters of the church is an entirely different one. It picks up and echoes and reverberates the whole biblical sound of God's movement to man: *He* stirs at Pentecost and newly creates the church and gives it unity because of his own love for man. He sets the solitary in families and visits the lonely. Be clear on this: he does these things, and not we. If he does not, then the church is a purely human invention, not worth so much of our hope and energy. If he does and we do not acknowledge it, we claim for ourselves what we ought not claim.

Enough of all this! "Everybody knows" about God's initiative. We have all been properly set in our place once again this morning and reminded of our insignificance and impotence. A fine thing church did for us today! It reduced us to mouse-size or worm-size and sent us back to apartments and hutches and houses. And we are now expected to act as if we are to overturn the world for the sake of God's love? If that is what the church service and this text and this sermon succeed in doing, we will be better off to disperse now: things can only get worse.

So, turn it around. Be clear on this: there are things that man *can* do. And what he can do has a great bearing on the context in which we celebrate Pentecost, appreciate the church, and enact the meaning of our Christian unity. What man can do is not in contradiction to what God has done; our saying that he can do things is not an attempt merely to give equal time to the other side of the question. We have an entirely different obligation. We have to be faithful to the actual picture of the church in Acts, Chapter 2. It tells us what man can do.

As we study the text and listen to it, we detect a most interesting rhythm. First it takes people and spirals them to a center, where the Word is preached. This is the *centripetal* movement of Pentecost. Then it takes people and spirals them out from a center, where the world is reached. This is the *centrifugal* movement of Pentecost. A helpful tip: keep this movement in mind and you will have a convenient listener's outline of what I propose to say today and I shall try to do you the courtesy of sticking to that outline.

I

The centripetal movement, the spiral inward. The first verse tells us: "While the day of Pentecost was running its course they were all together in one place." "They" were the same scattered people who had hidden on a Friday and Saturday not long before. They were people who had good reason to stay at home: care of families, shop-tending, fishing, plying trades, minding the children. They were gathered. They could do something and they did something: they located themselves where spiritual events were likely to be recognized at a time when they might pay attention to them.

128

Not that God always has to wait for our waiting. Sometimes he is described as tirelessly busy trying to get our attention: think of the repetition with which he had to grant Peter the vision that the good news was for all nations. Sometimes he has to deal with the stubborn or the passive and not merely the inattentive. Remember old Balaam? And, most delightfully, he could interrupt and cajole an Amos or a Moses or countless other people who were concerned with a plow or a flock.

More often than not, however, big things happened to people who did something, who located themselves when and where there might be occurrences. You cannot complain that no one plays croquet in the front yard anymore if you have moved to an apartment with a concrete square before it. You cannot bemoan the fact that the trains don't come by your breakfast window if your house is not located near the tracks.

The disciples, the faithful, were "all together in one place" letting Pentecost run its course. They were children of the old promise and they celebrated the fiftieth (*pentekostos*) day after the presenting of the first harvest sheaf of barley, the fiftieth day after the first Sunday after Passover, and by happy coincidence, the fiftieth day of the Resurrection and the new promise. "When suddenly . . ." They were there, doing all they could do. Then the Spirit of God did what God can do, and we know the story.

I don't suppose I need to haul in a blackboard now and draw diagrams to make my point. We have spiralled in from our scattered world: we are gathered, waiting, asking for God's stirring. Sometimes we forget about the meaning of all this. Sometimes we join those who say: "I'll sit it out. If the church is to be renewed and united, God will work it. Sooner or later I'll be notified and when everything is perfect and to my satisfaction I'll take part. I might cast an occasional critical eye toward Geneva or Rome or New York or wherever the renewal-and-ecumenical bunch gets together. I might even pay attention to the part my denomination plays, though I am a bit less eager to extend recognition to the congregation down the block and the fringe members of our parish." [The movement for Christian unity includes them, too!] When we speak this way, the chances are we also join those who complain that not enough is happening in the church today. We can tear our lesson from the first verse: be "all together in one place," ready for the "suddenly's" of the Spirit.

II

What do we do when we are together? By now we have learned how vapid the concept of mere togetherness is. We have had the advantages of fellowship advertised and we are unmoved. A Jewish comedian tells of the time when he had just joined a new synagogue. He was there long enough to have sampled its low-keyed togetherness, its trivial fellowship. A few days later he was approached by a man who wanted to sell him burial lots in the synagogue cemetery. "What are the advantages?" "You can spend eternity with those with whom you now share fellowship." "What!" said the comedian. "I'm sick of them here and now and you want me to be close to them forever and ever?"

The story is a bit cynical, but its punch and point are clear. Something has to be at the *center* when the spiral has spiralled, the magnet has drawn, the centripetal force has pushed people

130

together. Something was. Men talked. The ageless confusion of Babel and its separation was overcome. God spoke again through men. Here was no superficial or trivial man-centered mutual looking-in-the-mirror society. Instead there was immediately a concern for the language, the speech, the Word, the action of God. Recent events were in peoples' minds. Seared on their memories was the vision of Jesus Christ who had given himself for them so visibly. The preachers that day, adapting to the many needs of the hearers, spoke of the wonderful things of God.

Mere unity is not much of a goal. It can be attained best among people who stifle their creativity and thus eliminate conflict. This congregation would be most harmonious and united if we passed around a can of ether or drugged everyone. It is more difficult to achieve unity while people are alert, imaginative, contending for truth, active. They will inevitably clash, if they are thinking about themselves. But if "the great things God has done" interrupt our fellowship, we are in range of great new things. Lesson-without-blackboard number two: let's rehearse and talk about God in the middle of our world, the world where we live, where we have jobs and parties, the world where we seem to want to elbow Christ out of life and where he returns in dignity and suffering in our neighbors.

III

After the centripetal movement to the center, the Pentecost story immediately reverses itself. It turns its hearers and participants to the future and the furthest ranges of experience: "For the promise is to you, and to your children, and to all who are far away." This refers to what is called "ecumenism in time

131

and space." You and your children represent the great things God does and will do. Those who are far away represent the world-wide Church and the world-wide world. This is the *centrifugal* movement, the spiralling out of Pentecost.

This outward push can be destructive of unity. People become divided and separated through distance. They forget, as the generations pass. They have private and personal experiences and become captive of their culture. They invent little human things that are not even anticipated in this story: denominations and churches and sects and cults and traditions. But if these forms are not all anticipated or even fully compatible with Pentecost, they do not annul the promise through the ages and into all places. People dispersed after Pentecost.

There came the time that day, too, when people returned home. They blew out the candles and lamps and looked ahead to a workweek. They packed their bags for long trips back to the countries where seventeen different languages were spoken. Some went to forget; some were baptized and they went out to announce the promise.

Did their going out, their mission, compete with their being "all together in one place"? Today we hear that unity and mission must be in competition. The self-confident competitive denominations do the mission work and the tired, gentle churches talk harmony and concord. We may find that this is how churches act in the world today, but we know that the competition or contradiction is not built into Pentecost: it is the result of our misinterpretation or wrongdoing.

The Christians who talk unity without mission do not want the world to take seriously the promise for all; those who talk mission without unity do not want the world to take seriously the moral and theological claims of the church. Lesson number three is so obvious now that we need not state it. So I won't.

IV

When they *dispersed,* they did not merely disperse. First at Jerusalem and then around the world "they met constantly to hear the apostles teach, and to share the common life." Christian fellowship and unity are portable. But the local units are not independent. Oh, I do not mean that we have to care about the quality of the gym floor at First Presbyterian or the state of the budget at Grace Methodist or the bowling banquet at St. John's Lutheran Church. We do not have to busy ourselves with every detail of every denomination. Maybe some of these things deserve our studied disinterest.

But "sharing the common life" does commit us, without waiting, to a most concerned and profound life together. Again, God alone creates unity. But we can do something. We can get out of the way of his movement and let ourselves be swept up in it. We will inevitably be drawn together, not for mere togetherness but for his working of his purposes. We can speak of "every man being his own ecumenical movement" here and now. We have an ear on the apostles' teaching, an eye in the common life: that still leaves an ear to hear the world and an eye to look toward the world's needs and its interests. Pentecost calls us not merely to unity or to truth: it calls us to salvation, which means Christ's own wholeness and health, his fulfillment in our love as in his cross.

IF WE ARE ALL ON THE LEVEL

by VINCENT P. McCORRY, S. J.

Retreat-Director, New York Province, Society of Jesus, Shrub Oak, N. Y.

"Being therefore exalted at the right hand of God, and having received from the Father the promise of the Holy Spirit, he has poured out this which you see and hear."

—ACTS 2:33

It makes an extraordinary phenomenon that men should be fully aware that they stand at one of those significant points in human history where an entire epoch or era is ending and a new phase or period is beginning.

The age of the Reformation and Counter Reformation is over. A particular *zeitgeist* is dead. As religious man looks back over the last four hundred years he may well feel the sting of embarrassment and even the deeper pain of shame. The point is, however, that at this blessed moment of a new Pentecost we will all gladly turn to the future rather than brood upon the past. No one knows now what name, in the annals of history, the new era will bear. We might hope that it will be known as the age of Christian unity.

In the sixteenth century, Christianity, which, as an institution, had already been gravely wounded by division in the East, suffered an all but mortal blow in the Reformation. To argue now about the rights and wrongs of that sixteenth century split in the Christian edifice would be only to renew the dreary and disedifying polemics of four hundred years. In the fifteenhundreds something of magnitude took place. Whatever the nature and intent of that shock, its issue was division. Worse yet: its issue was holy war—and in that terrible phrase you read the full horror of four centuries of Christian contradiction and self-contradiction.

The institution most severely damaged by the Reformation was the Roman Catholic church. Inevitably that institution developed certain characteristics in the centuries that followed.

Moral bodies so often act and react exactly as physical bodies do. Slashed to the bone, Roman Catholicism has been convalescing since the sixteenth century. Now when a wounded or sick man is convalescing, he is not (as the word itself postulates) in possession of his full strength. Indeed, the convalescent is not truly himself. He is recovering, but he is not recovered. He is in neither sense what he was, and not yet what we hope he will be.

What is perhaps more important, for all this long time Roman Catholicism has been largely on the defensive. This is not to say that the Roman church, attacked, did not as fiercely attack. Again, let us not engage in the bootless and pointless effort to tote up the score in the holy war. It is simply a fact that post-Reformation Catholic theology developed chiefly as an answer and even as a polemic. Furiously assailed on grounds and in areas where she never dreamed of being challenged, Rome flung her devoted partisans into the breaches that had been made—and kept them there, not noticing, at times, that the attackers had fairly well ceased to attack.

Again, a person who stands habitually on the defensive is not truly himself. After recent outbreaks of physical violence in the New York subways it was observable that when a subway train stopped at a station, riders looked up nervously to see who would enter the car now. Such anxiety is not characteristic of urban commuters. Being on the defensive, these people were not truly themselves.

It cannot be denied that the Catholic church has for long cultivated a habit of exclusiveness and separateness. We really do not claim the habit as a virtue. We do identify it as a defense mechanism.

The further consideration is that defensiveness breeds hostility. People who are under attack will very soon feel that they are being most unjustly used, all the more as the tormenting accusations seem to them more slanderous. Once more it is not necessary to suppose that all the hostility lay on one side. Any fair-minded person must be revolted now by the shocking abuse poured upon the Roman church by the American journalism and nativist oratory of less than a century ago.

At any rate, the most obvious trait of the Christian world for the last four hundred years has been intramural hostility. Hostility produced its most immediate and perdurable effect: an almost total breakdown in communication. Catholic and Protestant studiously avoided one another, especially on the ecclesiastical level. Hostility simply froze, dislike became instinctive, all inescapable contacts were marked by uneasiness, painful correctness, and shameless brevity. The result of all was horrendous: a mutual, bottomless, glacial distrust.

Thus we arrive at what is the single plea and purpose of this present communication. If the day that now dawns is to be in truth Joel's *day of the Lord . . . that great and notable day,* if it is indeed to be the era of the Holy Spirit and of Christian and religious unity, then one imperative condition must be fulfilled in all of us who stand on the radiant threshold of the new time. We must trust one another.

The Roman Catholic is reared on dogma and authority, he is bred on what he takes to be the most literal and immutable absolutes. There is a certain danger—and it exists not only on the popular level—that for the adherent of Rome the new ecumenism will mean this. We Catholics, doctrinally correct as we are and harshly used as we have been, must now be more polite and flexible than in the past. We must handsomely acknowledge our apparent errors and excesses, and must give the impression that we are re-examining both our own and the Protestant position. We must allow, in matters of small moment, what previously we had refused to tolerate. We must courteously accede to the contemporary cry for communication. When we have generously complied with such requirements of the time—what is that old proverb about honey, vinegar, and flies?—our Protestant friends will very soon begin to see the error of their ways. In a trickle at first, then in great waves, they will come 'round, or rather, they will "come in," they will "come back." So it must be; *because these poor people cannot really believe what they say they believe.*

If such a travesty be the ecumenical outlook of any representative sector of Roman Catholicism, then that mutual trust which we take to be the primary postulate of the new age is doomed from the outset. We cannot ask Protestants to trust us if this be our thinking, for such ecumenism is not a spirit, but a gambit. We cannot ask our "separated brothers" to have faith in us, since we obviously have no particular faith in them and their intelligence and their good conscience. The most deadly Catholic suspicion of Protestantism has been the rooted suspicion of insincerity.

Surely it is not wide of the mark to propose that on the American scene no one man has done more to advance true ecumenism than that late and universally lamented Jesuit Father Gustave Weigel whom so many of all persuasions counted as their faithful friend Gus. It was the privilege of the present commentator to observe Father Gus at close range as he went tirelessly about his unifying task. And always, as he watched and marveled, this person thought to himself again and again, "But they all *trust* him! That is the secret. Protestant, Catholic, Jew—all trust him. They *know* he is on the level."

In this new and wondrous age the loving, unifying Spirit of God will surely bend down to us all—if we are all on the level.

TAKING THE CHRISTIAN GOSPEL
TO A NON-CHRISTIAN WORLD

by ROBERT J. McCRACKEN

Senior Minister, The Riverside Church,
New York, N. Y.

"The field is the world."

—MATTHEW 13:38

"Go therefore and make disciples of all nations,
baptizing them in the name of the Father and of
the Son and of the Holy Spirit, teaching them to
observe all that I have commanded you; and lo,
I am with you always, to the close of the age."

—MATTHEW 28:19-20

The familiar sentences from Matthew make one thing very
plain. The faith we profess had from the start a world outreach. What happened on the day of Pentecost indicates that
there was nothing parochial, provincial, or exclusive about it.
Those to whom it meant most knew that it was too good to
keep to themselves and must be shared with men and women
everywhere. Christianity in its essence is a missionary faith. It
simply has to testify to the truths which it believes to be world
truths, truths which can liberate, save, and unite all mankind.
World-wide witness is the purpose for which the church of
Christ exists. If Riverside Church were not in its life, organiza-

139

tion, and outlook a missionary church it would have little claim at all to the name of a church.

First of all, then, reflect upon what the church of Christ in its world outreach seeks to accomplish. Missionaries don't go overseas to coerce people to become Christians, to impose the Christian religion on them, far less to promote Western culture or Western standards of living or Western democracy, or, as one person put it, "to turn good Buddhists into bad Baptists." Missionaries go overseas without any assumption of superiority and without arrogance, to learn as well as to teach, to learn before they begin to teach. They are appreciative of all that is best in the spiritual heritage of other peoples, and they are aware that they are not taking Christ for the first time to any people because there is a latent Christ in the hearts of men and women the world over. A woman in central Africa, hearing a missionary for the first time, said when he finished speaking, "There! I always told you that there ought to be a God like that."

To express the matter briefly and succinctly, the church of Christ in its world outreach seeks to *witness,* to witness to Christ, to bring people face to face with him, so to speak of him and so to live and work for him that people will be persuaded of his reality. What this presupposes—and it is quite a presupposition—is that Christ is of supreme worth to us, is so great in our total view of things that we cannot think of keeping him to ourselves, but must share him with all mankind.

Concerning the missionary enterprise, there are facts that as members and adherents of the church you ought to know. You will not read about them in the newspapers for, in the nature of the case, they carry little detailed information about Christian missions. You can read about them in religious periodicals, in denominational magazines, in an interdenominational journal

140

like The *Christian Century,* but I doubt whether one Riversider in fifty subscribes to, and regularly reads, literature bearing on the subject of missions. It would be gratifying to have it proved that I am wrong in that estimate. I think it is incontrovertible that the average churchgoer knows startlingly little of what is going on in the world-wide church.

For example, we all know that the Christian gospel has been carried to every continent, but do we really appreciate the extent to which Christianity is a minority movement in the world at large? In Japan, not more than one person in two hundred is a Christian. In Pakistan, Christians are considerably less than one per cent of the population. In India, they are probably little more than two per cent. In Muslim countries, Christianity has made slight headway—the whole of Iran, for instance, having fewer than five thousand evangelical Christians. In East Asia, there are areas with as many as five to ten million people who have neither heard the gospel of Christ nor have had a church built amongst them. We sing with enthusiasm:

> Jesus shall reign where'er the sun,
> Doth its successive journeys run,
> Till moons shall wax and wane no more
> His Kingdom stretch from shore to shore

but with the birth rate going up every year in Asia it is sobering to come across the statement, as I did in preparing this sermon, that there are more non-Christians in India now than there were when William Carey settled there in 1792. On the other hand, there are certain African tribes more thoroughly Christianized today than are the urban metropolises of America and Europe.

As members and adherents of the church of Christ you also need to know, or to be reminded, that these are days of exceptional difficulty for Christian missions. China, the most populous nation in the world, has closed its doors to missionaries. In many countries—Turkey is a case in point—Christianity is no longer free to evangelize. The new nations want teachers, doctors, agriculturists, but, with the nationalistic sense strong and the old historic religions in some quarters experiencing a revival, there is antipathy toward "missionaries." It is distinctly possible that within a few years some of the younger churches in Asia may be cut off from the help of Christian churches in Europe and America. The nationalism that is astir in the new nations is frequently proving as unfriendly to Christianity as Chinese communism has. Some time ago at a Nairobi rally a Kenya nationalist leader asked, "Do you want missionaries here?" "No," yelled the crowd. "Yes," he shouted back, "they must be our houseboys." Rabble rousing stuff! And it is the kind of thing that is working like yeast in a ripe dough all through Africa and Asia.

You need to know too, or to be reminded, of the battle that is going on between Christianity and communism. For speed and spread, the advance of communism in the last forty-seven years is perhaps unparalleled in the history of any other movement. We have to acknowledge that it, not Christianity, is the major contender today in the battle for men's minds. It has many of the characteristics of a religion and for great numbers of uprooted intellectual Asians and Africans and South Americans it fills the vacuum caused by their inability to subscribe to ancestral faiths. It offers them an object of devotion, a philosophy of life, a program of action. It has been called "the fastest growing religion" in the East. Its agents, its missionaries are chosen for "nervous toughness" and are subject to rigorous discipline. They persistently pose as the foes of colonialism, as the friends of oppressed peoples, as being sworn to eradicate caste, class, and color discrimination, as being concerned to promote indigenous culture, art, literature, music. Lands of Christian missionary activity are their special targets. Make no mistake about it, the communist missionary movement is well planned, skillfully organized, heavily subsidized. Communist literature, cheaply priced, is flooding the East, whereas Christian literature is a trickle and priced above the financial capacity of the millions who are just becoming literate.

Jesus once commended a dishonest steward for his astuteness. Are the children of this world wiser in their generation than the children of light? Are atheists more determined and dedicated and resourceful in prosecuting their world mission than Christians?

For those of us who have genuine Christian concern and commitment all this is sobering, but there is another aspect of the case, a brighter and positive aspect. Christian influence has been far greater than the statistics suggest. Christ has made an impact on all the great non-Christian religions. Mahatma Gandhi was profoundly influenced by the New Testament, and many saw a manifestation of the spirit of Christ in his identification with the untouchables in India and a manifestation of the cross in his death at the hands of a fanatic who hated him because of his attempt to reconcile Hindus and Muslims. A missionary tells of a Japanese Buddhist for whom "Christlike" was the natural epithet, and of a Japanese woman, head of a school in Osaka, who said that she had become a Christian through association with him. I met a business man in South India, a practicing Hindu, who told me that he went every morning early to the great temple in Madura to pray, and who also told me that the Jesus of the gospels had time and again spoken to his heart.

Moreover, there can be no doubt that the gospel of Christ, carried to non-Christian lands, has exercised a tremendous social and political influence. I recall a dinner at International House with the guests of honor delegates to the United Nations. Three African delegates, on learning that I was a Christian minister, separately volunteered the information that they had their first schooling in a Christian mission. There are leaders of the new nations who testify to the formative influence of Christian beliefs upon the revolution in their lands. And well they might. Think of Livingstone's attack on the slave trade in Africa, of the campaign against opium, foot-binding, and concubinage in China, of the witness against caste, widow-burning, child-marriage in India, of the attack on disease, illiteracy, superstition, and of the schools, hospitals, and orphanages in one land after another. The spiritual roots of the tremendous social revolution that is taking place in Asia and Africa are in the soil of Christian social teaching.

You should know that in Christian missions new methods are being adopted to match the new day. The most notable of them is the attempt to secure that the church of Christ in every land shall be indigenous, that is, that it shall recruit its ministry from its own people, share fully in the life of its own nation, and while maintaining fellowship with Christians in the West, be free from all Western control.

Missionaries overseas are everywhere needed but they must be missionaries of a new order—not paternalistic leaders, not trainers of leaders, but servants, utterly identified with the people to whom they go, resolved to be thoroughly at home in, and to belong to, the land to which they go. "Come to us," an

144

African Christian said "to be in the church like salt in the meat." Another said that the identification should be "not a merely anthropological identification, but an identification in Christ." "Send us missionaries," the younger churches are saying, "who will be one with us, live with us, work with us, die with us, and lay their bones with ours."

The Peace Corps is attracting for social service overseas some of the very finest members of the rising generation. Surely the Christian church can attract young people from its membership who will unreservedly devote their lives to the service of Christ overseas. A congregation of our size should regularly, even yearly, be recruiting volunteers for a lifetime of work and witness in Africa, Asia, and South America.

There are two outstanding needs. One is the need for young men and women, teachers, nurses, doctors, ministers, who will offer themselves for missionary service. This type of report from overseas is typical. "We began the year in Guiana with two vacancies." Or this: "There are only three missionaries in the whole of Tobago." Or this from a city in North India: "I am the only missionary in Moradabad." The gospel of Christ is to be proclaimed to the uttermost parts of the earth. It is not being proclaimed to the uttermost parts of the earth. God has need, urgent need, of men and women.

Money is the other outstanding need. The work of Christian missions is always being hampered and impeded because of the want of money. Our fellow-Christians overseas are not able to do anything like what they could do because of financial starvation. We spend so much on the home base where we are over-churched and, by comparison, so little in the areas where support is desperately required. When I was in the Far East in 1957 I saw American military hardware, American economic aid, American military men, American business men, American

145

tourists, American films—usually of third-rate quality—American illustrated magazines featuring our abundance, crime, and social debauchery. The high priests of secular evangelism, the advertising agents and the high-pressure salesmen, were swarming all over the place. The missionaries by comparison were few in number and operating, financially, on a shoestring.

Look at the matter the other way 'round. Representatives from the younger churches in Asia come to New York, see the Interchurch Center, Union Theological Seminary, and The Riverside Church, and tell themselves what they could undertake if they had anything like our resources. Will you think about this? Will you talk about this? Will you talk about it in your organizations? Will you make an inventory of what you personally contribute in any year to the Christian missionary enterprise? And as you do your thinking and stock-taking, will you remember that world-wide witness to Christ is the reason for the church's existence? The field is—not Morningside Heights, not Manhattan, not Greater Metropolitan New York: "The field is the world."

TRIUMPHANTLY UNITED

by J. QUINTER MILLER

Associate General Secretary for Special Services,
National Council of the Churches of Christ in
the U.S.A.

"Until we all attain to the unity of the faith and
of the knowledge of the Son of God, to mature
manhood, to the measure of the stature of the
fullness of Christ."

—EPHESIANS 4:13

Many thoughtful people are troubled by the divided character of our world. The war in Southeast Asia, the struggle in
Cypress, and the stalemate in the negotiations for the limitation
of armaments at Geneva reveal the tragic divisions among the
nations. The desegregation struggles in Mississippi and Harlem
portray the deep cleavages among the races. The sectarian
character which persists among certain congregations and the
wasteful rivalry resulting therefrom in many local communities exemplify the tragedy of denominational division. The
nuclear, electronic, and space age discoveries which now furnish
the military means of racial suicide on a global scale make survival problematical. These are some examples of the serious
divisions around us. They present mankind with a summons of
compelling urgency: Unite or Perish.

147

In the midst of these conditions, the churches of Christendom are growing together in a remarkable way. They seek more fully to manifest their oneness in Jesus Christ. The Interchurch Center on Morningside Heights in New York furnishes one visible expression of our growing unity. On the marble facade, facing the main entrance, at 475 Riverside Drive, are carved the words:

"There is one Body and one Spirit just as you were called to the one hope that belongs to your call—one Lord—one Faith—one Baptism—one God and Father of us all, Who is above all and through all and in all."

The Bible assures us in the letter to the Ephesians that it is not the will of God, who made this universe, that it should be perpetually divided, but that it is his gracious purpose to bring all things in "the fullness of time into harmonious unity in Christ." The Christian church, as the body of Christ, is one. All Christian churches in New Testament times and today, with the rich diversity of their life, are the local manifestation of a single redeemed people. For the writer of the Ephesians, the fundamental division was between Jew and Gentile. The saving work of Christ, Paul asserts, has overcome such religious differences and may also overcome the denominational differences around us today.

There is in this, as *The Interpreter's Bible* asserts, "the pledge of a unity"[1] that is destined to grow until, in the words of my text, "we will attain to the unity of the faith and of the knowledge of the Son of God, to mature manhood, to the measure of the stature of the fullness of Christ" (Eph. 4:13).

Christians today are becoming triumphantly united in faith in Jesus Christ. The National Council of Churches illustrates

[1] See *The Interpreter's Bible* (Nashville: Abingdon Press, 1953), X, 605.

148

this fact. This unity is preeminently of the heart and mind and spirit. Encompassed by the tragedy of the world's secular life, Christendom as a whole is becoming triumphantly united.

Laymen and women often ask, rather impatiently at times, "Why don't the Christian churches get together?" Today our answer is, "They are doing just that in a magnificent way." The National Council of Churches now provides thirty-one communions, representing more than forty million Christians, with a living expression of their unity in faith and action. Thirty-nine other communions share in the work of the Council. Altogether the communions that carry forward phases of their work through their National Council have over 82 per cent of the nation's Protestant and Eastern Orthodox membership. And, since Vatican II, a new spirit of friendship and open dialogue with Roman Catholic brethren now pervades much of American Christianity. There is a notable degree of unity conveyed by these facts.

Many years ago I did not understand or accept this degree of unity within the Christian church. As an entering student at Boston and Harvard Universities, I doubted whether any one who was not of the Brethren faith could get to heaven. Some of you may know churches where similar doubts still exist. But God had a lesson for me to learn.

In order to earn my seminary expenses, I had to work. I was appointed Minister of Education at Trinity Episcopal Church of Newton Center, Mass. Here, as I worked with my Sunday School teachers and parents, I awoke one day to the realization that the Christian men and women of my teaching staff were just as Christ-like as any I had known in the Pleasant Valley Church of the Brethren. In succeeding years, this same realization has become a conviction concerning many other evangelical communions as I have worked with them. Because of our togetherness in Jesus Christ, his gospel of love and redemptive power can be preached and taught and lived and shared.

The ecumenical movement significantly shows that the church exists through these multiple denominational families as a dynamic and living fellowship—truly a community of the sons of God across the world.

In the full consciousness of this blessed achievement, let us turn now to consider areas in which Christians are becoming more united:

I. *Christians are united in their mission.* Christ calls us to mission and unity. There is always an urgency about the concept of mission. We are sent on a mission. The compulsion is the "still small voice" from within. We do not expect to realize full unity in faith among Christians, in the sense of organization or creed or church polity. Rather, Christians must be united in their mission in the sense of one consuming loyalty to the whole task in the whole world. We seek unity in obedience to the will of Christ. The churches' united work emphasizes their functional unity of purpose, and heart, and spirit.

It is the mission of the church to achieve that oneness for which Christ prayed—"in order that the world may believe." *Oneness* is necessary in order that the church may complete and fulfill her mission. As Emil Brunner has said: "The church exists by mission as fire exists by burning." All Christ's followers are called to mission and unity. This call in turn enables every branch of the church to share gloriously those treasured gifts and graces which are peculiar to its spiritual heritage.

Some of these treasures, like other Christian traditions, were the glory of their time in history. But loyalty to a denomination is justified only to the degree that its present day witness is vital, creative, and redeeming in this hour of our people's need. To each of us our churches must look to help preserve their tradi-

150

tion and loyalty. This, however, can be done only as we are loyal to the one Lord of the church. When any denomination becomes exclusive, separatist, and sectarian, then it becomes a liability to the wholeness that is in Christ.

As Christians unite to fulfill their mission, the Christian fellowship is strengthened within society. The gains are psychological and spiritual even where there is no perceptible theological change. Because of the living witness, which is now needed, the mission which our churches are called to fulfill is this: the faith we profess must correspond to the measure of the stature of the fullness of Christ.

II. *Christian communions are united.* Christian communions are united in the National Council of the Churches. This National Council is a thoroughly representative and evangelical body. Communion representatives constitute the council, determine its policies, and direct its work.

The basic significance of the National Council lies in its testimony to the fact that Christians "being many, are one body in Christ and individually members one of another." The council has no authority over any church but through its representative character and its democratic processes of voluntary co-operation, it increasingly draws the churches closer together in mutual helpfulness and in a united witness. The council is convincing evidence that we can maintain the principle of freedom, which is inherent in the gospel and was reaffirmed by the Reformation, while at the same time securing the practical unity which our times demand.

Although the program of the council is many-sided, its central role is simple: to be the servant of the churches as they seek, in their relations both with one another and with the general public, to act like one family of Christian people instead of isolated or rival groups. The council is not trying to create unity

151

(only the Holy Spirit can do that); it is trying to manifest a oneness which already exists because of our common relation to Christ as the one Head of his church.

The thrilling story of the Christian work the churches accomplish through the National Council cannot be briefly told. The scope of their combined ministry is so comprehensive and world-wide! But some illustrations of this work can be shared:

1. There is the pioneering *ministry of evangelism in 31 national parks*. In one year, 140 worker-ministers from theological seminaries and colleges served a quarter-million persons through providing services of public worship in the inspiring temples of God's out-of-doors.

2. Summer after summer, more than a quarter-million *agricultural migrants* have found release and happiness in worship, recreation, classes, and fun-sessions through the churches' ministry to migrants as they follow the sun and crops from Florida and Texas to the Canadian border. A massive assault upon bad living conditions, which for decades have beset some of these laborers, has been launched by the churches through their National Council.

3. The *revision of the Bible and the Apocrypha* has been completed and six publishing houses are now licensed to publish and distribute the Revised Standard Version throughout the world. Particularly notable was the action in 1963 authorizing the R.S.V. to be used by Roman Catholics in Great Britain. Thirty-seven communions now use this version in their teaching work. It is an interesting fact that since the publication of the R.S.V., it has been used in every denominational hymnbook of which we are aware.

4. *The application of Christian principles to economic life* has received prime attention in the work of the Council. Under the title, "The Church in a World That Won't Stand Still," Christian laymen have been engaged in the study of the following issues:

The influence of technology on family and community behavior
The role and responsibility of the consumer
The impact of technology on work, employment, and worker-management relations
The massive and monopolistic effect of economic power
The United States' economy relation to the world economy
The questions relating to the use of basic resources

Currently, special attention is centered upon the churches' role in the war on poverty.

5. There is a *need for expression of Christian concern on crucial issues.* The council's General Assembly and General Board alone can do this because it is in them that the churches' official representatives congregate. The churches feel a moral obligation to do this because all things are under the lordship of Christ. The council has declared itself: in opposition to Communism; in favor of expansion of international aid and trade; in favor of desegregation in education; unalterably opposed to all forms of segregation in the life of the church and society; in support of the United Nations; in support of the right of collective bargaining, both by employer and employee; and in urging the United States, preferably through the United Nations, to extend greater assistance to underprivileged peoples of the world.

6. The *utilization of mass media*—radio, television, and films—for the glory of God comprises the council's work in broadcasting and films. Broadcasts have totalled

153

19,409, over 227 radio, 291 television, and 32 armed forces stations annually.

7. The *nation-wide Program for Peace,* directed by the Council's Department of International Affairs, has been described by a State Department official as "the most effective instrument for world peace in America today." This work is receiving special attention by means of peace seminars conducted this summer at the Church Center for the United Nations and which have proven particularly timely for the crowds in attendance at the New York World's Fair.

8. The *helping of people to become literate* is a basic world thrust of the council's work. Forty-four per cent of the world's population cannot read. The hunger of people to read is almost inconceivable to us, who have always known how to read. An old man in the hills of Kachin, in northern Burma, who had never had a chance to go to school, learned to read through some of the young men who had gone down country to study under the literacy program, known as "World Literacy and Christian Literature." He walked 90 miles to the missionary's house and asked for the book which tells about God. The missionary asked him whether he wanted the little book or the big one. He said he wanted the big one. After walking back home the 90 miles, he began to read the book, seeking the name of Jesus but could not find it. He was on the third reading when someone came to his village who could tell him that what he wanted was the New Testament whereas he had only the Old. Again, he walked the 180 miles. When he returned home with his New Testament, he read about Jesus and said, "I believed immediately." He became a Christian pastor.

9. The churches also carry forward a co-operative *ministry of compassion*. Since 1950, the denominations, working through the Council's Department of Church World Service, have given material aid which has relieved the suffering of more than 10,000,000 persons in 50 countries in all parts of the world. Over 7,000,000 persons in countries overseas have had to depend on the American churches for some food every day in the year. One hundred and thirteen thousand former refugees are "homeless no more" because they have been resettled during the last 12 years through Church World Service. America's Protestant and Orthodox churches in a single year shipped 356,321,175 pounds of relief supplies through Church World Service for distribution to hungry, homeless, and destitute people overseas.

10. A notable *service to Americans living abroad*—600,000 of them—is extended through 200 English language union churches, 87 of which are directly related to the council. The Union Church at Teheran, Iran, provided an excellent example of its international character on a recent Sunday when worshippers put into the offering plate Indian, Lebanese, Egyptian, Italian, English, and Iranian coins plus two local bus tokens.

11. The fellowship and creative ministry of *United Church Women*. "Assignment Race" has been one important program area in which the united witness of church women continues to be focussed in helping to eradicate racial segregation.

12. *Long Range Planning*—Someone has said: "Time is a straight line of purposeful change in God's plan." The population explosion, population mobility, speed of transportation, the teen-age restiveness, the new leisure,

and larger numbers of elderly persons remind us of some significant areas of change. How do we prepare for the church's work in the decades ahead when there may be: a five-hour day, a three-day week, and a six-month year? Our member churches, nationally and by states, are now engaged in comprehensive long-range planning concerning what God wants his church to be and to do.

From these examples, you can see that Christian communions are united in their national witness in a magnificent way.

III. *Christian congregations are increasingly united in their community witness.* The truth of this is suggested by the attention the churches are now paying to the urgency for Christian unity in the locality. While unity in faith has frequently been glimpsed at local, national, and world-wide levels, we are convinced that now it must and can be experienced by the members of each local congregation. This is happening among us to a heartening degree, for the divisions by which churches are known across this nation are by no means as real as they appear to be. More and more, the churches are convinced that the local congregation's relating of its work with neighboring congregations is altogether basic. Here our oneness in Christ becomes operative and effective. Here the brokenness of persons in our culture must be made whole. God's purposes for his children are largely thwarted or fulfilled within local communities. A surer and more competent knowledge of the religious needs of people in neighborhoods is, therefore, utterly essential.

State councils have now been organized in every state in the Union except three: South Carolina, Mississippi, and Idaho. There are now 983 state, city, and local councils of churches; 336 of them have paid executive leadership. There are approximately 1,500 men and women devoting full time to the co-operative work of the churches. The budgets of these councils totalled approximately $18,000,000 in 1964, and is increasing at the rate of over $1,000,000 per year. There are, in addition to nearly 1,000 councils of churches, 2,251 Councils of United Church Women; 2,605 Ministerial Associations; and 152 Councils of United Church Men—a grand total of 5,991 state and local agencies of Christian co-operation.

Faith and Order is a relatively new dimension which beckons with promise. "All in Each Place—One" is a dream not to be denied! Christ is one. From the earliest beginnings, Christ's followers were felt to be one in him, sharing in a life derived from him.

A classic description of the nature of the unity we seek is the New Delhi affirmation of the St. Andrews Statement by the World Council of Churches: The unity which is both God's will and his gift to his church is one which brings all in each place who confess Christ Jesus as Lord, into a fully committed fellowship with one another through one baptism into him, holding the one Apostolic faith, preaching the one gospel and breaking the one bread, and having a corporate life reaching out in witness and service to all! And which at the same time unites them with the whole Christian fellowship in all places and all ages in such wise that ministry and members are acknowledged by all, and that all can act and speak together as occasion requires for the tasks to which God calls his people. (Adapted.)

The Holy Spirit, we believe, is leading the churches to sense their unity in Christ. He is helping us all to know that "when all parts are working properly, the Body of Christ is up-builded in love."

Christians are not divided, really. If we will only recognize the fact—the unity Christians have in Jesus Christ is deeper than their divisions. Wherever this truth is lifted up, in love, there the Body of Christ is strengthened. God, the Holy Spirit, is leading the churches into greater unity in him.

THE CONTINUING PRESENCE

by J. ROBERT NELSON

Fairchild Professor of Systematic Theology,
Graduate School of Theology, Oberlin College,
Oberlin, Ohio; Former Executive Secretary,
Commission on Faith and Order, World Council
of Churches

I

It was nine o'clock in the morning on the Jewish festival day of Pentecost and people suspected Jesus' disciples of being drunk. What else but inebriation could explain the strange behavior of the men who had lately followed the crucified rabbi? Having lost their leader, they were drowning their sorrows in new wine. Thus they babbled like men possessed of spirits. This was not so strange. Had not Jesus himself been chided by his enemies as a drunkard and glutton?

Peter answered the charges of the suspicious onlookers. The disciples could not be drunk; after all it was just the middle of the morning! But it was not alcoholic spirits, nor even evil spirits, which caused this unique event to take place. It was the long-awaited descent of the Holy Spirit of God. The ancient prediction of the prophet Joel, known to many of the mockers in the crowd, was at last being fulfilled. The more recent prediction, known only to the disciples for the past two months

159

since Jesus had promised that God would send the Holy Spirit, was likewise being realized before their eyes. So also in the tongues of flame, which seemed to play about their heads, was the prophetic word of John the Baptist fulfilled. He had declared that the one coming after him would baptize in Spirit and in fire. And this was it!

The Pentecostal wonder had still another meaning. The sad dispersion and estrangement of sinful men from God and from one another, as retold from generation to generation in the legend of the Tower of Babel and the confusion of languages, was now in Jerusalem being brought to an end by the Christian Galileans who spoke the tongues of "every nation under heaven."

On this decisive day, long-anticipated and always remembered, there came to dwell with men the Spirit of the living God as his continuing presence. He was the same Spirit who had brooded over the chaos of creation; he had spoken by the prophets; he had empowered Jesus the Christ to live his unique and redemptive life. Henceforth mankind could never be the same as before. The task of the disciples, and of all Christian people in succeeding ages, was to tell other men and women why the day of Pentecost was an irrevocable turning point in man's history.

Often we hear it said that Pentecost was the "birthday of the church." This is only partly true. The church did not *begin* then. God had called his people to be his own human instruments of salvation many centuries before. Redeeming God's people, the Son of God had chosen his community's nucleus some months before. So the church was in embryo until its true birth on Pentecost. Or, as some would prefer to say, the church was not born but was baptized on that day. From that day forth the church drew its "breath" and was constantly "in-

160

spired" by the divine Spirit who, like the wind in Jesus' analogy, could blow where he willed.

Men and women who, like all creatures, had been born of the flesh were henceforth enabled by God to be "born of the Spirit." It was the Spirit who enabled persons to speak out the gospel of Christ. He, again, gave power to the hearers and converts to make the all-important confession of faith, "Jesus is Lord." The Spirit incorporated the believers into Christ's continuing life through the act of baptism. Unto them the Spirit gave his gifts for their personal well-being and for the upbuilding of their communal life. Henceforth the "fruit" of the Spirit's work was discerned in the love, joy, peace, patience, kindness, goodness, faithfulness, gentleness, and self-control of the lives of Christian people.

The Spirit continually helped them in their weaknesses; when they struggled to find the elusive word of prayer, he already was interceding for them. To those who had been divided from one another, as natural men are prone to be, the Spirit gave a new unity to be maintained in the bond of peace, until they should all come to the unity of faith in Christ.

To those who had been without hope and without God in the world, the Spirit granted a hope for the fulfillment of righteousness in Christ's kingdom. And the life-giving Spirit, by whose power Jesus himself had been raised from the dead, exerted the same power to give eternal life to all who believed.

II

As a special day of celebration and worship, Pentecost has been exceeded only by Easter in the esteem and practice of the majority of Christians through the centuries. This is a preference which is readily understood when we read of the work of the Holy Spirit as described in the New Testament, and when we reflect upon the indispensability of his presence in the church and the world today.

It is only by the Spirit's power that the gospel is preached and received in faith. Only when he is present and effective in a congregation does the true and distinctive life of the church become manifest through the scaffolding of ecclesiastical organization and the ornamentation of much so-called religious activity. Through the inner testimony of the Holy Spirit in our hearts and minds, the words of the Holy Bible become not only passages of literary beauty and counsels of moral guidance but assurances of personal salvation based upon God's forgiving love and vivifying power. Without the Holy Spirit, the church dies. Without the Spirit in the churches, our individual lives fall away from the sustaining grace of God.

In view of the eminence of the Holy Spirit of God and the inestimable importance of his having been given to the church at Pentecost in the year of Jesus' crucifixion and resurrection, it is difficult to understand why Christian churches have allowed the day to fall into misuse and disuse. In many European countries today the weekend of Whitsun or Pentecost, coming at the end of spring, is just a time for outings, excursions, and festivities which conceal its religious meaning. In numerous Protestant churches of America the day of the Spirit's coming has been ignored almost completely, perhaps because of the false notion that it is a "Roman" celebration. And this is all the less comprehensible when one notes that the churches which pay little attention to Pentecost are often the very ones which lay greatest claim to the "freedom of the Spirit."

Special days like Easter and Pentecost are important to us only insofar as they call to remembrance each year the mighty acts by which God the Father of all men has given us hope of new life on earth and eternal life beyond it. Therefore it was right and fitting that the presidents of the World Council of Churches, when they desired to choose a time each year to address the millions of members of the Council's more than two hundred member churches, selected Pentecost. This was the appropriate day precisely because the three main emphases of the Council and of the current ecumenical movement are those three chief dimensions of the Spirit's work. These are the *mission* of the Gospel, the *renewal* of Christian life, and the *unity* of the church in all the world.

III

In this time of world-wide upheaval, revolution, uncertainty, fear, and strife, we Christians are quickly learning that the mission of the church is far more than the concern of certain people vocationally engaged as missionaries in distant lands. The persuasive and unrelenting proclamation of the message of Jesus Christ, and the extension of the worshipping fellowship of the faithful, are clearly the business of every responsible Christian. It is no exaggeration to declare that the ultimate peace of this threatened human race may depend upon the effectiveness of the Christian mission. Likewise it is sure that the irresponsibility of one Christian or of one congregation may have an abiding and detrimental effect upon particular persons who might otherwise have heard and believed the Word of forgiveness and hope.

More and more it is being dinned into our ears that the rapid increase of the earth's population is a problem of first magnitude for economists, agronomists, health experts, and statesmen. But what does this annual increase of nearly thirty millions mean for the Christian faith? It means that we Christians, for the first time since Pentecost, are a diminishing minority in the world. We have always been a minority; but until now an increasing one. Now we are clearly diminishing hour by hour as the population grows.

With world communism on the march, with the ancient religions of Asia and Africa surging ahead with renewed vigor and some political support, and with the disease of Western secularism spreading like an epidemic, there is massed before the church a combined opposition of staggering dimensions. Certainly the lines of Christians would crumble and fall into retreat except for one thing alone: the continuing presence of the Spirit of God. In this day of fierce testing, when by human calculation the Christian faith seems to be a lost cause, the Spirit is really giving the church new power for advance in its mission.

As the ancient martyr of the second century, Ignatius of Smyrna, declared of the Spirit:

It is He which giveth utterance and eloquence in preaching the Gospel; it is He which openeth the mouth to declare the mighty works of God; it is He which engendereth a burning zeal towards God's Word, and giveth all men a tongue, yea, a fiery tongue, so that they may boldly and cheerfully profess the truth in the face of the whole world.

IV

The Holy Spirit's work today is seen, secondly, in the much-discussed renewal of the church's life in many congregations. He is the life-giver, not only to the individual but to the communities of the faithful in each place. It is God's will that each church should show forth the life of mutuality and abundant meaning which he has conceived to be proper for men and women. Every little "colony of heaven," whether a great city

164

parish or a tiny fellowship of villagers, needs constantly to be shedding the aspects of a natural, self-centered, competitive society, and manifesting corporately the life of Christ's love. Renewal in regular worship, mutual service, social witness, education, and joyful association are coming about by degrees through the participation of all members, men and women, children and youth, laity and officers, and clergy.

For all the varieties of functions and services in each congregation there are members with special gifts; and these have to be employed in the upbuilding of the community. But whence come these gifts and talents? Not from some natural aptitude nor from environmental conditions, but from the divine Spirit. All the gifts necessary for the growth and renewal of the church, wrote St. Paul, "are inspired by one and the same Spirit, who apportions to each one individually as he wills" (I Cor. 12:11).

In some congregations it may seem that the Spirit has withheld his gifts, that scarcely any members have the qualities needed for expressing the real genius of the corporate Christian life. Other congregations may seem to be brimming with unused talent. But plain experience has shown that the true vitality of a church is not guaranteed by the large numbers of its members nor by their diverse abilities. It is quite literally a matter of the Spirit. And a small body of faithful Christians, unsophisticated and poorly educated, can show forth by the Spirit's gifts what the church is meant to be.

V

The remembrance of the coming of the Spirit at Pentecost points, thirdly, to the unity of the church. It was the Spirit himself who seized the disciples and other followers of Jesus Christ and made them subordinate all other family and social loyalties to their participation in the life of the church. And it was only one church to which they were committed, for they could acknowledge the existence of only one church of Jesus Christ. "For by one Spirit," continued St. Paul to the Corinthians, "we were all baptized into one body."

In the present century, more than in any previous ones, we Christians are being led to overcome the divisive barriers of denomination, race, and class, which prevent the oneness of the church from being experienced and seen. In truth the effectiveness of the church's mission and the renewal of congregations are largely dependent upon the degree to which this unity in Christ becomes manifest in every land. Yet we deceive ourselves by thinking that church unity is something we can fabricate by our own ingenuity and industry. Unity is always a gift of God; he has granted unity in the life, person, and ministry of Jesus Christ; and he enables the churches to appropriate unity by their acceptance of the guidance of the Spirit.

Today that guidance is being given clearly and dramatically. The generations of divisiveness among Christians, when the Spirit was being resisted and grieved by men, have given place to the era of our coming together. The dissolving of national and social barriers, the suppressing of prejudice, the willing surrender of certain outworn confessional traditions, the coming together of the churches in councils, common enterprises, mission and church union—all these unexpectedly rapid developments of this century may be attributed justly and gratefully to the free working of the Spirit of God. No other explanations can satisfy.

So the Day of Pentecost reminds us that the work of God in the church and in the world is being carried forward by the continuing presence and power of his Spirit. It tells us that in our desire to advance the mission, renewal, and unity of the church we need look for no other essential resource than him who has already come to us. And our proper prayer, therefore, is not a complaint about our inadequacy, but the plea that we be not rejected as unfit for God's service.

And take not thy Holy Spirit from us!

WHAT CAN THIS MEAN?

by WILLIAM A. NORGREN

Executive Director, Department of Faith and
Order, National Council of Churches

"And they were all amazed and perplexed, saying
to one another, 'What can this mean?' Others
said contemptuously, 'They have been drinking!' "
—ACTS 2:12 (NEB)

In all parts of divided Christianity there are voices witnessing
to the presence and the necessity of renewal, reform, and reunion. Why is this happening? What can it mean?

It has been said that some of the most troublesome problems
of the Church are not fundamental problems at all. They are
"bewilderments" growing out of the plight of "the conservative in every man," who is "getting a harder workout than ever
before" and who strikes back at the changefulness that is caus-
ing his discomfort. It has been said, "It is difficult to reform; it
is maddening to be reformed." But the Christian at this junc-
ture of history faces the ineluctable fact of change on every
side. It is true of the society in which he lives, where the only
real certainty is that there will be change and that the pace of
change will increase. It is true of the church of his fathers, in
which, though the rock of the faith itself is to be held without
change, the circumstances wherein that faith must be delivered

and held are irrevocably altered from the times of his fathers. The conclusion to which we must be open is that *new forms* of response to the apostolic faith are required, as, indeed, they have been required in former times, that such new forms will be a sign not of the absence but rather of the real presence of God the Holy Spirit in his church, and that it is the responsibility of the Christian to prepare himself through thought and prayer for their emergence in God's own time.

The church, the people of God, may not indulge in romantic yearning for former times, be they the conditions or the church of the primitive Christians, the early councils, the medieval synthesis, the Reformers, the Counter Reformation, or the nineteenth century revivals. In short, we receive the faith from the fathers, and we receive indispensable truth from the history and tradition of the church, but we are called to be the stewards for this age of what God gives us. No one else can perform this function for us.

Our age, in spite of similarities to a recent or distant past, is nonetheless a new age, marked by the working of multiple forces. Let us look briefly at certain of the fundamental characteristics of our times, those at least which are related to Christian unity, in order to see our task more clearly.

One of the most striking aspects of our age is the unity of the world, which seems to have grown small. It is not only that words and pictures are transmitted more rapidly and widely by television and radio, that the cinema, drama, and music are shared everywhere and are becoming the common inheritance of all, and that all airports look the same wherever the increasing body of international travelers penetrate. It is not only that universities are becoming internationalized, and that even in the traditionally sundered world of theology there has been an emphasis on catholicity. To these facts must be added the rise

169

of a new generation with new hopes and zeal, the arbiters of new unities, impatient with provincialisms and holding new ideas. Yet these are people who remain in their traditional surroundings, attached to their various ways of life and expression, and are concerned to create unity while preserving the kind of divinity which is the source of creative capability. People are being brought together in a community while preserving their originality, and this is a potential source of richness.

Yet, despite such persisting and creative diversity, it is certainly true that, whereas up to a short time ago humanity was divided into a large number of distinct national cultures, today a Japanese town is not essentially different from one in America, Europe, or South Africa. What once were separate national cultures are being absorbed by a uniform technological civilization which, while leaving individual languages intact, seems to have become a species of language common to all humanity. The terms of this language are coined by the American-European technological civilization. We have arrived at a unification of humanity parallel to that achieved by the Mediterranean world in the time of Jesus under the influence of Hellenic civilization and the pax Romana.

This "opening to Christianity" is, however, not so propitious as it might seem; for Asiatics and Africans in particular, but others as well, have observed that two thousand years of Christian history have been filled with cruelty, intolerance, battle, and bloody persecution of those who did not share the same faith. They do not distinguish between the practical shortcomings of Christians and the fundamental rectitude of Christianity itself. Instead, they discount Christianity, draw an unfavorable comparison with the tolerant spirit of India, are drawn to the Buddha that expresses renunciation and forgiveness, and to the heritage of the Koran. There is a revival of ancient religions,

170

and this is associated with a limited revival of the various national cultures with which these religions are associated.

All this, plus the lessening of the influence of western culture in relation to that of Africa and Asia, has had an effect on the mind of Christianity. Formerly, Christians were too much inclined to attribute an absolute value to the cultural heritage of the West. This made it easier indeed for them to believe in the absolute character of Christianity. The opening up of new horizons has removed many an illusion from Western man, and has made him aware of the limits of his own culture and historical background. This has been beneficial in the sense that it has helped him to understand the relative and mutable nature of all purely human forms and institutions and to acquire a sense of humility in which he no longer attributes an absolute character to his own human historical heritage.

It has, above all, helped him to distinguish the true absolute from the confines of the pseudo-absolute, and has helped make it stand out in all its genuine purity. But it also exposes Western man to the dangers of a relativism that, unconsciously touching even Christians, is one of the characteristics of our time. It is when relativism denies every absolute value, acknowledging only what is relative, that it becomes a real negation of faith.

But enough has been said about contemporary directions in the world to illustrate our point that change is its characteristic and that such changes, it would appear, have a bearing upon the forms in which the church may deliver her unchanging faith.

The church always lives under the impulse of the Holy Spirit. The last half century of her history has been a particularly fruitful period. It is this resultant situation—the fruit of a new life—that now, increasingly, needs to be clarified. The church is experiencing a pause just now, perhaps a very creative pause. There seems to be a deep inner struggle. Someone has

171

said that its manifestation is "a mood of concerned impotence."

The church senses that something is going on, and that it must have a part in it, but cannot for the moment see how to go about it. Experiments are made, churchmen try to get next to the secular man in the secular world, not to save him out of it, but to experience it with him, to struggle with him in the midst of it. There is new sensitivity in the church about the world. On the academic side, the growth of the historical method of studies, which led to the revival in biblical and patristic studies, the theological recovery, the liturgical movement, and the ecumenical movement itself—all are signs of what is happening in the church.

In the ecumenical movement, the old defensive approach of interweaving traditions for the sake of stemming the tide of secularism is waning, as is that of cultivating an aesthetic delight in each other's heritage for the sake of some democratic ideal of harmony. Forces are being assembled for moving out in common mission in the new world. The youth of the church in its interdenominational assemblies, perhaps the most sensitive of all Christians to the changing society in this present age, are increasingly demanding of the church and of their elders, more relevant theologies and social statements, less pretension and less defensiveness. The requirement today is that the church take up a role of genuine leadership, confident in the power of the living Christ.

So long as the church is content to live for itself, to turn its back upon the world and merely defend what it has, it can find sufficient reasons for being disunited. But when the church takes seriously its responsibility to evangelize the world, then disunity among the messengers of the one Christ becomes unbearable. When the messengers of one Lord are unreconciled to one another, how can they proclaim the one reconciliation in Christ

172

for the whole world? Into what are we inviting all men—a new complex of divisions in place of their own? These questions bring us deep into the issues of faith and order that divide us. We are concerned, primarily, not with the number or size of our ecclesiastical structures but with the integrity of our witness to Christ, that men in every place may hear the authentic voice of the one Shepherd of the sheep, undistorted by racial, cultural, and denominational divisions.

People are confronted with the ecumenical movement today in a way that they were not even a short time ago. The denominational rationale has been badly broken. It is difficult to find a theologian who will defend the denominational pattern as it now is. Even the Roman Catholic church has been shaken by this. Indeed, for the first time since the Roman Empire, all portions of Christendom have at last been brought to the point of contact and have embarked upon a dialogue. In this dialogue we hold the mirror of Christ's gospel up to one another, as a test both of ourselves and of our partners. In this way, the things that we regard as essential are brought home to others, and at the same time we are given the possibility of new critical insight into our own teaching and life, which will lead to a meeting, on our part, of their essential requirements—all of this with a view to unity. The discussion of differences does not mean peace but, theologically speaking, the sword. But the clash of doctrines is essential to progress. This is a radical movement which reaches the depth of our problems and which means struggle and painful theological repentance before there can be a new vision for the church.

Movement toward Christian unity is manifold, complex, and difficult to predict, but one point emerges with unusual clarity at this time: No matter how remote unity in faith and order may be, the unity of *all* Christians in charity, concern, and common action cannot, and need not, be delayed. Even though separated bodies of baptized Christians continue to exclude one another from the Holy Communion and full church fellowship, they may yet be able to live together as divided churches in the one Christianity. It now seems possible to find such a temporary solution to the question of Christian unity by which the churches would be able to transform the historical division of the churches of the Reformation, the Eastern Orthodox, and the Roman Catholic into a genuine spiritual togetherness, although the divisions between these churches continue.

It would appear that a sufficient doctrinal basis for such Christian solidarity is to be found through the exploration of the implications of our common baptism into the Body of Christ and the several other elements of unity which persist within the separated communities. This is the epochal step which is being taken today. There is no impossible theological barrier to a fullness of common service, a joint theological enterprise, and joint economic, social, and educational action, based upon our common baptism. And this is as true of the local community as it is of national and world spheres. The difficulties now lie in practical implementation and the psychological reorientation of the various separate communities of Christian people.

Unless we go forward to meet those who also bear the sign of the cross, and if necessary "go the extra mile," we will be guilty of denying and attacking Jesus Christ himself. This is all the more true if we should fail now to go forward and meet those who are advancing towards us. The more our Christian brothers appear to us to be unattractive, willful, or in error, the more we must strive to love and understand them. Nothing less can satisfy the demands upon us of the love of God, which characteristically manifests itself upon the cross. The Christian and the churches must, like their Lord, empty themselves,

174

accept death and accede to the hope that they may rise again in the power of the Holy Spirit. Old structures, forms, and conceptions will be crushed then by the pressure of God, and the new gift will be given.

PREPARING FOR THE ECUMENICAL PENTECOST

by CECIL NORTHCOTT

Editorial Secretary, United Society for Christian Literature and the Lutterworth Press, London; and Editor at Large, The *Christian Century*

"Men of Galilee, why do you stand looking into heaven?"

—ACTS 1:11

I stood recently on the so-called Mount of Ascension, the little knoll on the Mount of Olives overlooking Jerusalem where this dramatic question was put to the amazed disciples. Whether the question was put on that spot matters little—geography has never been a boundary to the Christian faith. But what is important is the contention that the Ascension experience was essentially a Pentecostal one with the company of disciples grouped round the kingly presence of Christ and already beginning to move into the spiritual power of the upper room. This mount of the Ascension foreshadowed Pentecost.

From the Mount of Olives you get the best view of Jerusalem —the city in which the Christian faith first began to understand something of the mission of the church, an experience which is always developing and is never finished. Christ often used the Mount of Olives as a retreat but he always came back to the city. It was in the city that he died and it was there that Pentecost happened. But the balance between the mount and the city is an important one in the development of the Christian faith and, in particular, of the ecumenical movement. The key to it lies in the words of the text.

These disciples were Galilee men, and, of course, there is a tradition that the Ascension experience happened in Galilee itself. But the power of these words lies in the fact that they were spoken within the orbit of Jerusalem, the capital city of the Jews, the hub of the Roman government. These men of Galilee were bidden not to contemplate the glories of the view of the earthly powers surrounding them, nor the heavenly powers that could be theirs but to remember Galilee. It was there that the power of the risen, ascended, and glorified Christ was to be used—it was there that the coming Pentecost was to be seen.

This Ascension experience could have turned the men of Pentecost into a set of skyward-looking, starry-eyed idealists who might happily have been received into Judaism as another group of fanatics and eccentrics to fade out of existence as, in the course of time, the memory of their Jesus also faded. This experience on Olivet could have maintained its dazzling brightness for a few years, but it was doomed to disappear unless the men got off the mountain and remembered that they were "Men of Galilee."

Like an electrical system Christianity, if it is to work, must "earth" its faith. It may have the most elaborate wiring system imaginable, but unless there is the skilled and continuous contact with the "earth" the system is dead from the start. It is true that some skyward-gazing is both useful and necessary, and some happy nostalgia is not dangerous provided you don't live by it. But to "earth" your faith in events, in people, in countries, in vocation, in politics and history is of the very

177

stuff of the faith. Without this "earthing" Christianity is just a group of idealisms, and the church becomes a ghetto of like-minded people.

To be caught merely "looking" is a supreme danger for Christians and from which, at various turning points in time, they have been providentially saved. The Ascension-Pentecost experience, and the charge to be "Men of Galilee" is one of the saving points in the history of the church. I believe that the present ecumenical movement with its emphasis on Christian unity is another one provided we are aware of the challenge that the Ascension-Pentecost experience brings to it.

G. K. Chesterton, the English Catholic writer, once said that if you wanted to make any movement "living," then you must make it "local." It must have its roots where people live and work. A movement of leaders and conferences will always have a certain artificial influence and power but the real power lies in the people—in Galilee, and in all the Galilees of the world!

I often pass through the little English village of Tolpuddle, a little group of cottages in Dorset, and my eye always lights on one of them in which James Loveless lived in the early nineteenth century. A simple farm laborer, Loveless, with five others (some of whom were Methodist preachers), dared to form the first trade union in order to get a living wage for themselves and their families. For this offense they were transported to live in the then wild and distant Australia—practically a banishment for life. Loveless and his friends were the "Men of Galilee" of the early trade union movement. They translated hopes, dreams, and talk into action—almost at the cost of their lives. Their Pentecost was a bitter and cruel experience, but they anchored it in the cottages and fields of this little English village and from it grew the immense structure of trade unions that we know today.

Don't stand looking into heaven! It is a temptation for all Christians and for all Christian movements and, in particular, the movement for Christian unity. The Pentecost power is too often felt to reside in conferences, assemblies, and world gatherings in the great capital cities where the so-called leaders of the churches meet and make pronouncements. All this is part of the Ascension-Pentecost experience, but the essential element in unity and the growing together of the churches lies in its local manifestations.

1. *Christianity is a local religion and Pentecost is tested by its local power.* The present emphasis on the international character of the Christian church and of the universal aspect of its life should not blind us to the important fact that it is also a local religion. It began in Galilee and stepped on to the universal stage in Jerusalem with a powerful warning note not to forget Galilee.

And it is this warning note that we must hear and obey today. The description of the various peoples and languages at the first Pentecost is a reminder of this local power which glories in diversity rather than uniformity and is able to marshal the world's languages within its compass and so give substance and peace to the Tower of Babel.

This sense of Christianity's local power is at the heart of the missionary movement which has carried the gospel across the inhabited globe and made disciples of all peoples. The early pioneers struggled with the languages, translated the scriptures, and gave the faith a local context and contemporary character. Their zeal was not generated in world conferences and assemblies although it might have taken on a more cohesive strategy if it had been! No, their zeal was essentially a local and even a lonely one. It bred individualists who were inclined to go their own way in spite of what missions secretaries six thousand

179

miles away might try to say to them in letters which happily took six months, at least, to reach them.

Although Pentecost gave power to the whole church, the emphasis of early Christianity was on the "churches" and the individual flavor which each of them developed. The churches in Antioch, in Alexandria, in Rome, in Jerusalem, and in all the great cities of the world that Christianity gradually made its own had their individual character. The common faith did not mean a pallid uniformity but a lively determination to discover and develop those aspects of the common faith which might have a local flavor. In other words, the early churches made Pentecost local and by doing so made it living.

It is just here, I think, that the right word should be said about the inheritance of local life which comes to the whole church from the separate companies of churches. We rightly decry the divisions of the church today, and the swing of the Christian tide is in the direction of unity, and in that we rejoice. But the individual gifts of the churches do enrich the whole church. The Holy Spirit is not inactive even in the separate companies of Pentecost, and the power today of the ecumenical movement comes partly from the riches of the separated groups. The great family groups of the church have discovered, even in isolation, that faithfulness to a confession, a conviction, or a principle is not to be regarded as a sin against Pentecost but rather as a loyalty to the Holy Spirit. We do a disservice to the whole Christian church when we lament the separations of the past as if lamentation was the only activity called for. We should rejoice in what the separated companies have discovered by making the Christian church a truly local church, and rooting it in the national, cultural, and language areas of the world.

The ideal of one Holy, catholic, Apostolic Church, toward

which we strive today, would not be attainable unless we had behind us the long years of local Christianity with its treasures of intimate relationships with local places, countries, climates, and cultures. In many places, unfortunately, they have hardened into barriers, but the ecumenical movement is surmounting those barriers and, what is more important, is bringing the truths of the separated companies into the great church that is now growing before our eyes. In many ways ours is a greater Pentecost than the first experience in Jerusalem, for we have taken to heart the challenge of the Ascension that we should not simply gaze into heaven but take the gospel into Galilee. This leads to the second point in this discussion of the power and purpose of the ecumenical Pentecost.

2. *Christianity is an amalgam of dialogue and decision.* This is particularly true at the present time when all the doors of the Christian church are open wide and we go in and out of each other's houses with a freedom that would astonish churchmen of an older generation.

We are discovering the truth that Pentecost is composed of a continuously widening range of understanding, and that we do this by dialogue and decision, and by doing so, we receive power. The first Pentecost was not just a free gift. It had to be prepared for by an obedience of mind and purpose. What happened at the Ascension experience was a preparation for it, and so is the present range of contacts between the churches. When I look down the long calendar of ecumenical events each year, and contemplate the time and energy spent in meeting, conference, discussion, and debate, I wonder at the truth of what I have just said. Can all this be genuinely part of the dialogue between the churches which must prepare for, and precede, the coming great Pentecost? I believe it is, although at times one

181

is doubtful about the worth of some of the meetings which appear to be arranged by professional ecumenists for other professional ecumenists!

But in the main, the present dialogue and meetings are vital contributions to the modern ecumenical Pentecost, and without them we cannot expect a visitation of the Spirit. They are part of the ministry of locality. They bring the issues of church disunity into the arena of discussion and debate instead of leaving them in lonely and frigid isolation.

I had this brought home to me very vividly in an experience recently in the Belgian Benedictine monastery of Chevetogne. This community is dedicated to the Pentecostal task of healing the deepest wound in Christendom—the division between the Eastern and Western churches. To me, a Western Protestant, and almost totally ignorant of the great Byzantine Church of the East, this healing process has always seemed remote and as otherworldly as the divine liturgy of the Eastern church itself. But the men of Chevetogne have made it local. While gazing into heaven through the magnificent ritual of the Eastern church these Roman monks of the West are also understanding students of the East. They celebrate the two rites of East and West and open their community to guests of all churches who will come in the spirit of enquiry. Their Pentecost is already beginning within their monastery. They believe that by prayer and worship with understanding and knowledge they can contribute to the healing of Christendom. They are part of the dialogue and decision that offers Pentecost at any time we are willing to be obedient to the call of the Spirit.

How much this needs to be practised in the great city and urban areas of the world, where the separated companies of Christendom live alongside one another for generations and know very little about one another's worship, theology, and general life. We are too content inside our little church ghettoes. We have become localized groups while the true locality of the whole church is there waiting to be realized in a local Pentecost.

We can decide to institute our own form of dialogue and make the decision which could lead to our local Pentecost. There is no need to stand looking at what church leaders do in ecumenical debate and conference. Ours is the arena of the true dialogue and decision, the place where the church becomes one not only in word but in deed. We are Men of Galilee wherever we live, and the call to be truly Pentecostal and ecumenical in our own backyard is the central message of Pentecost to us today.

3. *The Christian Church today is a foreshadowing of the Great Pentecost to come.* The great truth that the present generation of Christians is learning is that no form of the organized church is final in its form and style. It is true that forms such as episcopal, presbyterian, and congregational will always have a place in the outward form and order of the great church to be. They have won their recognition not only by scriptural authority but by usage over hundreds of years of time. But if we are truly heirs of Pentecost, we dare not worship outward forms and regard them as sacrosanct and unalterable. That is gazing up into heaven and refusing to be Men of Galilee! The Holy Spirit is showing new ways for the church to be organised, and new understandings of what is meant by the ecumenical movement.

We are not called in the ecumenical movement to join church to church, organization to organization in a magnificent turn of ecclesiastical joinery as if by joining things together we could fashion a new church. The church is not made in that fashion. The ecumenical movement is called upon to an obedience that is far deeper than any such operation. It is nothing less than the shaping of the great church-to-be, the divine company whose form and order are laid up in the heart of the Holy Spirit who, by various ways, is now showing our generation that the great church is the gift of the Spirit and not the foundation of ingenious men.

For many this is hard and forbidding news. We are all anxious to close the ranks of the churches and to present to an increasingly secular world a common front which will appear, at least, to suggest unity. We grow impatient at the slowness of unity, and exasperated at what seem to be the small differences that divide the churches. But it is just at this point that we need patience. It is when the churches appear to be very near to one another that we need to be on our guard and to be sure that the unity we hope for is also of the Holy Spirit.

I may give an illustration of what I mean from recent church history in England. One of the forms of unity in England is the hoped for unity between the Anglican and Methodist churches. It seems, to anyone who knows the common history of the two churches, to be a natural move in closing the ranks of the churches. But there is a great deal more to this proposed act of union than meets the immediate eye. If this union could be accomplished there would happen in England a religious revolution in the form and order of the church which would change the ecclesiastical map of England, for this union fundamentally calls for a Pentecost that would issue in the creation of a new "Church of England." The Pentecost that John Wesley knew 150 years ago would be completed in the life of a truly national church to which perhaps all the people of England could give their devoted allegiance.

Now this hope is one that is hidden within the scheme of union. It is not set out in clauses and resolutions and there lies its greatest hope of accomplishment. To set out with that goal

184

would cause the hosts of argument and even opposition to appear far too early and perhaps decisively. But the hope is there. At the moment it is a Pentecostal hope. It could be described as part of the Ascension experience of looking into heaven and gazing into the starry distances. We can only correct that vision in England by bringing the hope into the localities where the Men of Galilee can get to work to turn hope into substance, and dreams into realities.

The great-church-to-be is not one to be organized by the ecumenical movement and its ancillary forces, such as the World Council of Churches, which in any case must be a passing phenomenon in the coming of the new Pentecost. Councils of churches are part of the scene of time, and the danger about them is that we regard them as organized aspects of church unity and we are content that this should be so. But councils of churches can be a stumbling block to unity. We can rest content with them and their notable achievements in co-operative work. But they are no substitute for unity. Only the church itself can be a foreshadowing of the Great Pentecost to come.

Here then is the challenge of our text. Councils and conferences place us on the Mount of the Ascension, and they prepare us for Pentecost. But we need to hear the potent conversation which terminated in the call to the Men of Galilee not to forget whence they came and what their duty was back home; that Galilee is wherever we live, and wherever we dare to believe that a new Pentecost of wonder for the Christian church is possible; and that we can help to prepare for it today.

SURPRISED BY THE SPIRIT

by RONALD E. OSBORN

Dean and Professor of Church History, Christian
Theological Seminary, Indianapolis, Ind.

"And suddenly a sound came from heaven like a
rush of a mighty wind."

—ACTS 2:2

"Awe fell on everyone."

—ACTS 2:43 (Moffatt)

God is constantly taking men by surprise. We see it over and
over again in the Bible. The very word *gospel* says it: here is
good news, totally unexpected and overwhelmingly glad. The
ministry of Jesus came upon men like that, so that the evangelist
was reminded of the ancient prophecy: "the people who sat in
darkness have seen a great light" (Matt. 3:16).

The birth of the Christian church stole upon a world off its
guard and left men struck with wonder. Recall the familiar
details of that first Pentecost after the Lord's resurrection: the
little band of disciples gathered with one accord for prayer.
Suddenly a sound from heaven. A rushing like a mighty wind.
Tongues like flames of fire. The apostles filled with the Holy
Spirit. Their speaking in other tongues, a speech understood by

men gathered from the corners of the earth. Mockery. Peter's sermon. The conversion and baptism of three thousand. Their joy in the common life of the church.

Although we have heard the story scores of times and know its phrases as well as many lines from Mother Goose, we would be hard put to it to describe in sober, scientific language what actually happened. What did men really hear or see or feel? Many of us must confess that we should be quite uncomfortable in circumstances like those described in Acts 2. Talk about being "bewitched, bothered, and bewildered"! That is just the way the author describes the Pentecostal situation. The multitude were bewildered, amazed, astonished, perplexed (Acts 2:6, 7, 12). God had taken them completely by surprise. They really did not expect him to intrude upon their lives that early morning in spring. But even more shaking, they did not expect the strange things that he did that day. The account of the first Pentecost is the story of men surprised by the Holy Spirit.

Is not this the message that comes through to us from the life of the early church? We are at a loss to say what really happened regarding the wind, the fire, the tongues. And yet the essential point is perfectly clear to us. The story of Pentecost dramatically focuses the typical action of the Holy Spirit—overwhelming God's people with new realizations of his grace in Jesus Christ, his universal redemption, and the community he creates through forgiving love. Such a realization awakens within us gratitude for the overflowing mercies of God and a readiness to receive the blessings of the Spirit which he is ever eager to bestow upon the people whom he has called.

Consider a little longer the familiar stories of the early church in the Book of Acts. It has been frequently said that the chief personage in Acts is neither Peter nor Paul, but the Holy Spirit.[1] Perhaps it has not so often been observed that the work of the Spirit characteristically takes men by surprise. Acts might well be called the Book of Surprises—the surprises of the Holy Spirit.

The book begins with a little band of believers clinging to a memory and huddled prayerfully over a hope for their Lord's return. Then the Spirit comes upon them, and to their surprise they find themselves proclaiming with power Jesus Christ as Lord in the living present. Their word is understood by hundreds. The company of believers becomes a joyful host, sharing a life of gladness and of praise.

At the beautiful gate of the temple a crippled beggar is surprised. He asks for alms, and in the name of Jesus of Nazareth he is commanded to walk. When the temple officials call in the apostles for investigation, they too are taken by surprise, for Peter is filled with the Holy Spirit, and his defense becomes a powerful testimony to the gospel. As the officials observe "the boldness of Peter and John, untrained laymen," they are filled with wonder (Acts 4:13). On the release of their leaders, the disciples assemble for prayer, "the place in which they [are] gathered together [is] shaken; and they [are] all filled with the Holy Spirit" (Acts 4:31). We must pass hastily over many

---

[1] Ph.-H. Menoud, "Holy Spirit," in J.-J. Von Allmen, *A Companion to the Bible,* (New York: Oxford University Press, 1958), p. 171.

who were taken by surprise: that wretched couple, Ananias and Sapphira; the jailers with the apostles under guard; the Ethiopian treasurer puzzling over an ancient prophecy when Philip appears to ask about what he is reading and to tell him the good news of Jesus Christ; the persecutor Saul confronted by the living Lord; Ananias of Damascus commanded to go to Saul with the gift of sight and the promise of the Spirit; the servant girl Rhoda tiptoeing out of the prayer meeting called on behalf of imprisoned Peter to answer a knock on the door and finding him standing there!

Now we must not conclude that Acts is merely a collection of wonder stories from a credulous age. For the surprises of the Spirit bring new realizations of the meaning of the gospel. Consider the quaint and colorful story of Peter's vision at Joppa. Trying to pray, he was distracted by hunger and drowziness— even an apostle must contend with such disturbances to the life of the spirit! Then, in a trance, he saw a great sail filled with all sorts of livestock and heard the command to kill and eat. He protested in shock: it would not be *kosher*. Nothing common or unclean had ever passed his lips. Then the voice: "What God has cleansed, you must not call common." The dream was interrupted by strangers inquiring for Simon Peter. And when they took him to the Roman centurion Cornelius, the message of the dream was clear. For as the apostle told of Jesus of Nazareth, the Spirit fell on Cornelius. In that moment Peter understood what the early church had to struggle so hard to learn: the church of Jesus Christ is a fellowship open to all men of faith, Jew or Gentile. Surprised by the Spirit, the church discovered its ecumenical character. The universality foreshadowed at Pentecost flowered into fact.

II

The surprises of the Spirit have not ceased. Again and again, as our Lord kept reminding his hearers, the overflowing mercies of God take us when we least expect them. He comes like a thief in the night, like the bridegroom suddenly appearing as the wedding party sleeps, like the master returning unexpectedly from a long journey, like the friend arriving at midnight. The point of half a dozen parables is that God, not man, chooses the time of his coming. Perhaps that is what it means, after all, to say that he is God. *He* rules the universe, not we—not even with our rockets and atom bombs. *He* determines times and seasons. We think we know where he is. We settle comfortably into our familiar patterns of life. And all at once he confronts us anew. Whether in blessings which we immediately recognize or in judgment, which is the preparation for his blessing, the Spirit takes us once more by surprise.

At no point are the surprises of the Spirit more dramatically evident in our time than in the rising tide of the ecumenical movement. From the day of the first Pentecost, the joyful sense of oneness among Christians has been recognized as a gift of the Holy Spirit. Indeed, the New Testament speaks of "the unity of the Spirit" (Eph. 4:3). How vividly this realization has been growing in our century.

There is nothing remarkable in our recognizing our oneness with those Christians who are like ourselves. Indeed, this feeling of belonging to a little introverted group of like-minded people is what the natural man tends to prize in our church life. Yet it is the bane imposed by the denominational system: we become pleased with ourselves and expect very little more from
190

God, except an occasional word of commendation and perhaps an attendance prize. But over and over again in all parts of the world the Spirit has been surprising self-satisfied Christians by a realization of their oneness with Christians very much unlike themselves. So have arisen the great enterprises of missionary co-operation, the fellowship of interchurch aid, the World Council of Churches, the National Council of Churches, state and local councils of churches, and actual unions among denominations. Particularly in Asia, where Christianity knows itself to be a tiny minority, has the movement toward united churches gathered strength.

Church union is not primarily a defensive maneuver to marshall all the Christian forces under one command. Any man of common sense can see the hardheaded, practical wisdom in that. But any churchman who has tried his hand at union negotiations can tell you of the problems which immediately arise, even among Christians of generous goodwill, in trying to resolve the issues which so long have separated us. Where the efforts have been successful, the participants unfailingly speak in gratitude, not for their own achievement but for the gift of God. For at some point in the discussions they have been surprised by the Spirit—first in an intense realization of their oneness in Christ despite all their difficulties and differences, and second in the emergence of a solution to their most stubborn problems. What great occasions of rejoicing have marked the institution of the United Church of Canada, the Church of Scotland, The (reunited) Methodist Church, The Church of South India, The United Church of Christ, and many more. The victory of God has surprised many a heroic congregation, which has discovered to its enrichment that the Lord also adds to his church men of varied races and hues of skin.

Many of us individually can testify to the personal enlargement of our own Christian understanding as we have worshiped with a congregation very unlike our own, using an unfamiliar liturgy and perhaps an alien tongue; suddenly, despite all our foreign awkwardness, we have been surprised by the Spirit with a strange sense of joy in belonging to these folk so much unlike ourselves and yet so like us at the deepest point in our life—the knowledge of God in Jesus Christ. This has happened to me in a Swedish cathedral, in a Swiss village church, in a Waldensian chapel high in the Italian Alps, in a Coptic church in Egypt. I have heard friends testify to being caught up in the spiritual mystery of the Orthodox liturgy in Greece or Russia. And many of us Protestants have come to know a sense of Christian kinship with our Roman Catholic brethren in the contacts which have newly opened in these recent years.

Any Christian who has been thus surprised by the Spirit has received a great spiritual gift. He is like the apostle Peter standing there at Caesarea overcome in wonder when the Spirit fell on Cornelius. God takes us by surprise. He opens to us a whole new world of spiritual reality. And he leaves us filled with unspeakable joy. The leaders in the movement for church union in our day are men and women whom God has taught not to despise any of his chosen.

III

Some Christians are afraid of anything which threatens to change the life of their church as they know it. They want no surprises. They tend to think of the word negatively: a surprise is an ambush, an unanticipated complication in our plans, interference from an unexpected quarter. If we are inclined to think thus, we stand in need of our Lord's admonition to become as a little child. Not only does a child trust his parent. He loves surprises. For the word means to him sheer delight, a gift he did not expect, offered by the hand of love. It evokes all the wonder and the joy of finding hidden treasure or the most precious of all pearls. Even the divine interruptions of our familiar routine, which so chill us to contemplate, prove to be God's way of adding new dimensions of gladness to our lives. So sang William Cowper:

> Ye fearful saints, fresh courage take;
> The clouds ye so much dread
> Are big with mercy, and shall break
> In blessings on your head.

An ancient Christian prayer (the collect for the Sixth Sunday after Trinity) breathes the spirit of childlike trust and joy in which the faithful ever look to the generosity of the divine Father. It addresses God as the one who prepares for those who love him "such good things as pass man's understanding." Then it implores the gift of love so that we may obtain the promises "which exceed all that we can desire."

In such a spirit of childlike trust, the church of Pentecost awaited God's next and glorious move, the suddenness of the sound from heaven. So today we look to his unfolding of his purpose. We walk the way of faith, and at every turn find ourselves yet once again "surprised by joy."

THE UNITY WHICH THE SPIRIT GIVES

by ERNEST A. PAYNE

General Secretary, The Baptist Union
of Great Britain and Ireland, London

"The unity of the Spirit . . . the unity of the faith
and of the knowledge of the Son of God."
—EPHESIANS 4:3, 13

One August Sunday a few years ago, I was present in the
cathedral on the attractive Mediterranean island of Rhodes.
Rhodes was visited by the apostle Paul on his way back to
Jerusalem from his third missionary journey. The island still
has many evidences of the presence there of the Crusaders. My
visit was in connection with a meeting of the Central Committee of the World Council of Churches. For the first time the
members were meeting in the territory of one of the Orthodox
churches, which owes allegiance to the Ecumenical Patriarch of
Constantinople.

That Sunday morning the Holy Liturgy of the Orthodox
was being celebrated in the presence of Lutheran, Reformed,
Anglican, Methodist, Baptist, and Congregationalist Christians
from many different lands, as well as several hundreds of the
local inhabitants.

The congregation illustrated the diversity of race and tradition now to be found within the Christian church. To many who
194

were there the form and content of the service were strange
and difficult to understand. Some were tempted to disapprove.
Some remembered that in several places where the Orthodox
church is strong it is difficult for evangelical Christians to worship and witness as they wish.

In the course of the service, however, the Bishop of Rhodes
preached. A big, bearded man, magnificently robed, he stood in
front of the holy doors of the ikonostasis or screen and spoke
about the Holy Spirit. It was a powerful and memorable
sermon. Afterwards I ventured to say to the Bishop that were
he willing to come to London and, without his ecclesiastical
garb, preach the same sermon in Spurgeon's Tabernacle, the
congregation would respond and say "That is what we believe
about the presence and activity of the Holy Spirit in the
church."

To many of the visitors in Rhodes cathedral that morning
the service came as a revelation of the glowing faith and devotion to be found within the Orthodox church. They understood
better the place in its life of the doctrine of the Trinity and its
emphasis on the Holy Spirit. Christians long and widely separated from one another were drawn closer together in understanding and fellowship.

At Pentecost we remember the descent of the Spirit on the
infant church. One of the chief gifts of the Spirit is unity.
Unity is, in the words of the New English Bible's rendering of
Ephesians 4:13, "inherent in our faith and our knowledge of
the Son of God." We are made one by our belief in Christ. For,
as Paul said in writing to the Corinthians (I Corinthians
12:13), "by one Spirit are we all baptized into one body,
whether we be Jews or Gentiles, whether we be bond or free;
and have been all made to drink into one Spirit." This drawing
together of those of different races and background is one of

the chief activities of the Spirit. There is one Lord, one faith, one baptism. There is one Spirit and it is his function to unite.

The word "unity" is often on the lips of Christians today. Strangely enough it occurs only twice in the New Testament, in the two phrases I have taken as my text.

But though the word "unity" is rare, the idea is constantly emphasized in the New Testament. It is found in gospels and epistles alike. The idea runs like a thread through the Acts of the Apostles. There in chapter 2 we have the account of the happenings on the day of Pentecost. The Holy Spirit came upon the little band of disciples in the upper room. They were "all with one accord in one place"; they were "all filled with the Holy Spirit": the crowd outside were "all amazed and marvelled"; and the sequel to the day was that "all that believed were together, and had all things in common." Note the significance of that repeated "all."

The Acts of the Apostles begins with this story. It goes on to illustrate the reconciling, unifying work of the Holy Spirit. The last chapters of the book are taken up with an account of how, under the constraint of the Spirit, the apostle Paul hastened back from his missionary preaching in Europe because he wished "if it were possible for him, to be at Jerusalem the Day of Pentecost." He carried with him gifts made by Gentile converts for the needy Christians in Jerusalem, the earliest record of Christian aid, a symbol of newly discovered unity, the unity which the Spirit gives, the unity which is an essential element in our faith.

"Ye are all one in Christ Jesus," said the apostle Paul to the Christians of Galatia (3:28), where many social, cultural, and religious differences had to be overcome and where the initial hostility and suspicion between Jewish and Gentile groups were strong. The same truth is set forth again and again in the

196

letter to the Ephesians. Jews and Gentiles, circumcised and uncircumcised, are "reconciled unto God in one body by the cross" (2:16). And these words find a parallel in the Fourth Gospel where it is said that Jesus died, not for the Jewish nation but, "that also he should gather together in one the children of God that were scattered abroad" (John 11:52). The fruit of the Spirit is love, joy, peace, patience, kindness, goodness, fidelity, gentleness, and self-control (Galatians 5:22). All these things presuppose a basic fellowship and oneness of life and purpose. The Holy Spirit actualizes, effects, and carries forward the reconciling work of Christ on the cross.

Paul was therefore deeply shocked when he learned that the Christians of Corinth had divided into factions taking the names of different leaders: Apollos, Cephas, his own name, even that of Christ himself—factions ranged over against one another. "Is Christ divided?" he cried. Can Christ really be divided in this manner? Is there not an absence of the Spirit, a grieving of the Spirit, a lack of true faith and real knowledge of the Son of God, if Christians are content to remain in separate and hostile camps set over against one another?

Dr. John Scott Lidgett, one of the outstanding leaders in British Methodism in the last generation and an architect of Methodist union said, with Christians of other than the Methodist tradition in mind: "Say what we will, and take whatever position we may, we belong to one another." That is the message of Pentecost and of the New Testament as a whole. Under whatever names Christians go, from whatever lands they come, to whatever race they belong, and however diverse their forms of worship and their polity, the fact that they confess Jesus Christ as Lord makes them kin.

But what have we to say to the history of the Christian church with its frequent controversies, schisms, separations, excommunications, and persecutions? It is surely very difficult to connect this strange sad story with what the New Testament tells us about the activity of the Holy Spirit.

Two things must be borne in mind. First, it is significant that in his last hours on earth our Lord made the unity of his followers a matter of prayer. While he was with them, he had kept them safe and united—all save Judas. He seems to have foreseen how difficult it was to become after his departure, how dangerous disunity would be for the Christian cause. That in those last agonising hours, with betrayal and crucifixion so near, these thoughts were uppermost in the mind of our Lord suggests that prayer for unity should be continually on the lips of Christians both in private and public. This is one reason why the Week of Prayer for Christian Unity, now so widely observed, is so welcome a development. Christians have not, in fact, prayed for unity as much as they should.

Secondly, Christians have often thought of the unity of the church in far too narrow and rigid a manner. They have tried to make it depend on acceptance of a creed, on obedience to a bishop, on a particular relationship to some civil power, on the practice of certain rites and ceremonies, on belonging to a particular race or class, on a certain alleged evidence of conversion. Do as we do, believe as we do, many Christians have said, and the church's unity will be secure.

But the effect of all this has been to exclude and divide. The aim has been uniformity, not the unity which the Spirit gives, the unity inherent in our faith and our knowledge of the Son of God. Many of the sadder pages in Christian history have come through failure to recognise "the manifold wisdom of God," his variegated, many-colored wisdom, and the breadth and majesty of his redemptive purpose.

The apostle Peter was at first reluctant to recognise that the Gentiles were included in God's purpose, as well as the Jews, and to see that "God has no favourites" (Acts 10:34, NEB). Even now there are those who would divide the church into racial groups and theological groups, forgetting that the unity which the Spirit gives is, in the words of the letter to the Ephesians, "mature manhood, measured by nothing less than the full stature of Christ" (4:13, NEB).

"The full stature of Christ!" Of recent decades each denomination has been challenged to seek, according to its own forms and doctrines, a clearer understanding of Christ and a closer walk with him. And at the same time all denominations have been challenged by the discovery of Christ's presence within other denominations. The discovery has sometimes been made in the fires of persecution, as in Nazi Germany and in the Soviet Union. It has sometimes been made in the course of theological discussion, or through sharing in one another's worship, as in the cathedral at Rhodes that August Sunday morning, or through common action as in Christian aid. That is why James Hastings Nichols is right in suggesting that a good definition of the modern ecumenical movement would be "a movement toward the Lord of the Church in whom alone is the Church's unity and catholicity."[1]

One of the pioneers of that movement was Nathan Söderblom, who became Lutheran Archbishop of Uppsala. When he was a young man he set down this prayer in his diary: "O God, give me humility and wisdom to serve the great cause of the free unity of Thy Church."[2] Note that he asked for: humility and wisdom. All too often pride and ignorance determine our

---

[1] *Church History*, XXIII (September, 1954), 275.
[2] Stephen Neill, *Men of Unity* (London: SCM Press, 1960), p. 26.

judgments and actions. What the Spirit gives, now as at Pentecost, is not uniformity but an ever enlarging fellowship based on a growing understanding of the breadth, length, depth, and height of God's love in Christ and his purpose for his church.

EXCITEMENT OR ROUTINE?

by DAVID H. C. READ

Minister, Madison Avenue Presbyterian
Church, New York, N. Y.

"Then they that gladly received his word were
baptized: and the same day there were added unto
them about three thousand souls. And they continued steadfastly in the apostles' doctrine and
fellowship, and in breaking of bread, and in
prayers."

—ACTS 2:41, 42

Not too many Christians today would associate the Holy
Spirit with the romance and excitement of religion. And to most
people outside the church the phrase, "Holy Spirit"—and still
more the ancient form "Holy Ghost"—symbolizes the dullness
and obscurity of our beliefs. There is an aura of vagueness
about it, and a faint smell of moth balls. Nobody would expect
to be thrilled by a lecture on the Holy Spirit. Even in our music
we reflect this attitude. When we want a quiet hymn to balance
a couple of rousing songs of adoration or Christian service, we
turn to the section marked "The Holy Spirit," where we normally find the dreamiest words married to the softest tunes.

Why this quiet, woolly atmosphere has surrounded the
thought of the Holy Spirit is a mystery. For in the Bible you

201

find almost the exact opposite. There the Spirit, both in the Old and New Testaments, stands for the dynamic of God's actual presence, the flooding of our everyday lives with divine power, the energizing of a flagging faith, the invasion of a sagging, debilitated society with new physical, mental, and moral strength.

In the most primitive stories of the Pentateuch it is the Spirit that possesses the heroes of the faith and inspires their mightiest deeds. Do you remember how Samson was delivered over to the Philistines, securely bound "with two new cords?" "And when he came unto Lehi, the Philistines shouted against him: and the Spirit of the Lord came mightily upon him, and the cords that were upon his arms became as flax that was burnt with fire, and his bands loosed from off his hands." This is typical of the Old Testament conception of the "Spirit of the Lord." The Spirit breaks into the normal pattern of existence and supplies the ordinary with extraordinary powers. A shepherd-boy becomes a warrior-king; a courtier becomes an inspired prophet of God; a rabble becomes a consecrated nation; the "dry bones" of the valley, visited by the Spirit of God, becomes "an exceeding great army."

Everywhere, when the Spirit moves, there is life, movement, challenge, hope, and opportunity. "The Spirit of the Lord God is upon me; because the Lord hath anointed me to preach good tidings unto the meek; he hath sent me to bind up the brokenhearted, to proclaim liberty to the captives, and the opening of the prison to them that are bound. . . ."

And that, you remember, was the word that was taken up by Jesus Christ when he launched his campaign in his native land. "And Jesus" we read, "returned *in the power of the Spirit* into Galilee: and there went out a fame of him through all the region round about." His attack on the evil powers that enslaved

202

the bodies and souls of men was made in the name of this energizing and renovating Spirit. "If I cast out devils by the Spirit of God, then the Kingdom of God is come unto you." The Fourth Gospel tells us how he prepared his followers to expect that same Spirit to descend on them and animate the church of God on earth; and the book of the Acts records the promise of the risen Christ: "Ye shall receive power, after that the Holy Ghost is come upon you: and ye shall be witnesses unto me both in Jerusalem and in all Judaea, and in Samaria, and unto the uttermost parts of the earth."

The first evidence of this breakthrough of spiritual power came on the day of Pentecost, when "they were all with one accord in one place." However we interpret today the "rushing mighty wind," the fire, and the speaking with tongues, it is certain that these men and women had an experience of inrushing divine power that not only transformed each individual, but welded them together into a dynamic community that set off on a fantastic journey through two thousand years of human history. Peter's sermon to the crowd that day seems simple enough but its effect was startling. "They were pricked in their heart, and said unto Peter and the rest of the apostles, 'Men and brethren, what shall we do?' "

And Peter was more ready to answer that awkward question than most modern preachers. "Repent and be baptized every one of you in the name of Jesus Christ for the remission of sins, and ye shall receive the gift of the Holy Ghost. For the promise is unto you, and to your children, and to all that are afar off even as many as the Lord our God shall call." There was surely excitement enough that day in Jerusalem. For "they that gladly received his word were baptized: and the same day there were added unto them about three thousand souls."

Well, what has happened to us? We celebrate Pentecost. We

are reminded that such things happened. We feel that there must have been some extraordinary motivation for this Christian movement that has lasted into the mid-twentieth century. We are prepared to stand up and say: "I believe in the Holy Ghost." But do we really experience—or even expect to experience—any breakthrough of divine power into our lives, any overwhelming sense of the actual presence of God in our Christian community today, any vivid signs of his action in our secular and scientific age? Have we not successfully domesticated Pentecost as a religious memory tucked away in a corner of the Christian year? We have somehow made the Holy Spirit the most distant of all God's names, when in Bible language he is, so to speak, the point at which the Trinity impinges on us here and now.

No amount of rationalizing can disguise the fact that romance and excitement, a vivid sense of supernatural power, has disappeared from most of our church life today. To be sure, we know all about the dangers of emotionalism; we are well equipped with psychological explanations of what used to be called "movements of the Spirit"; we have seen through the kind of religious excitement that evaporates in a piety that leaves no trace of moral determination to challenge evil in all its forms; we cannot forget the picture of John Newton composing hymns of devotion on the deck of a ship that was packed with Negro slaves. Yet doesn't our conscience tell us that there is something missing? Our religion is surely not meant to be merely a well-organized method of encouraging a belief in God and a friendly co-operation in furthering good causes at home and abroad.

What is missing is surely a redemptive power that we know cannot be found elsewhere in modern life—a divine reality that can illuminate the depths, fill the emptiness, and open our hearts to one another. Dean Samuel Miller in his new book,

EXCITEMENT OR ROUTINE?

The Dilemma of Modern Belief, has this to say about our churches: "Organization is a quick substitute for redemption. When two people are related—and it takes time, reflection, imagination for that to happen—then both are changed, whether they like it or not. In organization, people merely make contacts, and the result is that no one is changed. The redemptive vitality in human relationship is dropped out; there is not time for it. It is easier for a church to organize three thousand people than to redeem one of them."[1]

That last sentence made me stop and think. For we are so conditioned to organize that our first response is: True—then how shall we organize redemption? Shall we appoint a special committee on the Holy Spirit? Surely it is just at this point that we are thrown back on the real meaning of Pentecost. The church *was* organized—you can read about the various stages in the succeeding chapters of Acts. But it was organized as a channel of the Holy Spirit. God's spirit cannot be controlled by man. "The wind bloweth where it listeth." For us what matters is to believe that the wind will come, and to have the ship manned and the sails hoisted —not to be scooting off in another direction with our little outboard motor.

What this means is that for a Christian to know this redemptive power, for a church to be a community vibrating with the living presence of God, there is need for a routine as well as the moment of inspiration and excitement. What happened immediately after the tremendous experience of Pentecost? It sounds like rather an anticlimax: "They continued steadfastly in the apostles' doctrine and fellowship, and in breaking of bread, and in prayers."

Here is the routine of the Church's life—*for Jerusalem then and for New York and every other city at the present time.* The

[1] New York: Harper and Row, 1963, p. 65.

Holy Spirit means the energizing force, the vivid reality of God, the redemptive power—but this cannot be turned on at will, like a stream of water from a faucet. There are some signs today that Christians who are impatient with the lack of spiritual life in the churches will seek some group that claims more spectacular evidence of the Spirit's presence—miraculous healing, or speaking with tongues. It may indeed be true that such groups have appeared in our day in reaction to the terrible secularization of our typical church life, and we dare not write them off as cranks or fanatics. But the chief signs of vitality remain what St. Paul called "the fruit of the Spirit . . . . love, joy, peace, long-suffering, gentleness, goodness, faith, meekness, temperance"—the redemptive qualities that are not spectacular and cannot be organized. To receive them, to know this energizing power, there is a place to be—and that is mapped out for us in this picture of the church's apostolic routine—the doctrine, the fellowship, the sacraments, and the prayers.

In case you are now thinking that a sermon that set out with a promise of excitement, of a method of spiritual renewal, is now going to peter out with a recommendation of "the mixture as before," even threatening four new "heads" at this late hour—let me ask you if you really think of these familiar elements of the church's life as channels for the redemptive energy of the Spirit, if you really expect that the routine of the church could be the means of charging your life with new meaning, and transforming the society in which we live? Aren't we all tempted to look in some other direction for the refreshment and renewal so many are seeking today?

A famous German clown used to do a turn in which he appeared alone on a darkened stage. In one corner there was a brilliant circle of light in which he stood looking anxiously down. A policeman would appear and ask: "What are you looking for?" to which he replied: "The key of my house." "Did you drop it here?" "No—somewhere over there." "Then why are you looking here?" "Because it's dark over there."

There are many bright patches of light where we are tempted today to look for an answer which all the time we know in the depths of our hearts really still lies over there in the familiar shadows. The path of hope, then, for a church, or for you and me, is not a frantic chasing after every circle of light that flits across our stage, but a new attitude of expectancy as we follow the familiar routine.

What is it? The *apostles'* doctrine. Not some new speculation, propounded by someone with a special "hot line" to the Holy Spirit, but the gospel as declared by the men who had been with Jesus. It is this that can come alive in each generation. It is this, when preached and taught, that can still be the agent of spiritual revolution. The fellowship—not what that word has come to mean in our degenerate vocabulary, but the *Koinonia,* the community of men and women held together by nothing less than the Holy Spirit, the strong, supporting bond that we have only begun to explore. *The breaking of bread*— this is the Holy Communion that is the centre of the church's life. Here, and in baptism, we have to discover how a familiar rite can be the instrument of a supernatural invasion of our drab, mortal existence. And the *prayers.* When these first Christians met they prayed together. It was as they were praying, you remember, that the Holy Spirit fell on them with such astounding power. We have continued in this apostolic prayer. Together in worship we offer this same adoration, confession, thanksgiving, petition, and intercession. But what has happened to them? Are they crammed with the sense of God's presence, the expectation of his reply?

I believe that we all want to have a more vivid sense of God's reality, a genuine experience of the living Christ, a conviction in the bottom of our hearts about all the things we profess to believe with the surface of our minds. I believe we all want a religion that will generate ethical power in the world around us. I believe we all want a faith that lights up every corner of life, and not just a half-belief that is more a burden than a joy. All this means that we want the Holy Spirit. We want Pentecost. How much do we want it? Enough to stick with the old routines, even when, as we say, we don't "feel like it"? Enough to bring a spirit of expectation to our prayers and worship? Enough to look for the Spirit's presence in unusual places?—for we mustn't imagine that he is restricted to the routines of the church.

We celebrate Pentecost, then, not as a memorial of a distant divine event but as an expectation of a power to come and a realization of a presence now. None of us can live, or ought to live, in a state of religious excitement. But if we seek the moment of truth, the time of true inspiration and conviction that only God can give, then our task now is to be alert and to hoist the sails. And that means, among other things, that we shall "continue steadfastly in the apostles' doctrine and fellowship, and in breaking of bread, and in prayers."

PRELUDE TO POWER

by PAUL MINNICH ROBINSON

President, Bethany Theological Seminary,
Oak Brook, Illinois

There is an old story about a church burning to the ground, which naturally drew a large crowd of the curious from the community who had come to watch the blaze. The minister too was there and noted that never before had he seen so many people around the church. He spoke to one man standing by, "I don't believe I have ever seen you at my church before." The man replied, "Sir, I have never seen your church on fire before."

There is more sad truth than humor in these words. We cannot deny that the fervor and concern of the first century Christians is missing in most of the churches of the twentieth century. There is, among more sensitive Christians at least, a realization that with all of the architectural grandeur, efficient organization, theological sophistication, and general prosperity of most of our churches, there is something missing for which there is a genuine hunger.

I may have before me an electric motor, perfect and precise in every part. It may be well conceived and carefully put together, but it is useless until it is plugged into the source of electric energy which makes it an instrument of power. So a church may be informed and structured for her ministry, but without the power of God to quicken and enliven her best endeavor, she

209

is lacking the spiritual dynamism that makes her witness bold enough to change the world.

The book of Acts is certainly a tract for our times. The amazing story of the small band of dedicated disciples of Jesus Christ who in the face of persecution from the most powerful political force the world had ever seen not only survived, but demonstrated the power to change the course of history, has been a constant challenge to the church of every generation. It is a vain and nostalgic desire for the church today to seek to become "The New Testament Church" as some bodies claim to be. We must live in the twentieth century, not the first. Furthermore, anyone who thinks that the early church was perfect needs to read again the epistles of Paul. But the very life of the church today may well depend upon her openness to the power by which the first Christians lived and died, a gift which fulfilled the promise of the living Lord, "But you shall receive power when the Holy Spirit is come upon you; and you shall be my witnesses in Jerusalem and in all Judea and Samaria and to the end of the earth" (Acts 1:8).

This baptism of the Holy Spirit was no accident. The disciples had to be prepared for it. God will not entrust his power to those who are not ready for it. Perhaps this is one reason why our churches pray so vainly for the baptism of the Holy Spirit. Only a fool would entrust a high powered automobile to a child. So perhaps God has withheld the power of his Spirit from many in his church because we are not yet spiritually mature enough to receive him.

Note the way in which the first disciples were prepared for the experience of Pentecost. Perhaps in this prelude to power, we can discern the conditions by which the gift of the Spirit may come into the life of the church today.

When the apostles had received the commission to witness

210

to all the world, and heard the promise of the presence of the Spirit, they went down from the Mountain of Ascension to the upper room which had been their meeting place (Acts 1:12-13). Here they continued in *fellowship* with one another. They did not go their separate ways, each seeking a personal relationship with Jesus Christ apart from his brother. And the Spirit came upon the whole church and upon each one as they were within the community of faith.

The Kingdom of God has suffered too long from the lack of a clear doctrine of the church among many Christians. We are sometimes so impressed with the highly personal nature of discipleship and Christian commitment that we forget that as followers of Christ we are not set in solitary ways but are members one of another in a covenant community of God. Four times in the second chapter of the book of Acts, it is stressed that the disciples continued *together*. They were not only in relationship with Jesus Christ but with one another. When they were thus together, the power of the Holy Spirit came upon them.

Moreover, they were together with *one accord*. I am sure that this did not mean that they were agreed on every matter which came before them. The New Testament picture of the apostles would certainly indicate that they were men of independent judgment. But unity does not necessarily mean conformity. It does not require the elimination of difference of opinion. Unity is the spirit which binds men together in spite of difference.

A family at its best is made up of individuals who are held together not by a common opinion, but by a common love and loyalty for each other. Members of the family do not always think alike. They may differ in tastes, interests, and even in convictions. Yet a family, free to express individual differences,

211

may experience a remarkable kind of solidarity because of their love for one another and their devotion to their common cause.

I think this kind of oneness has much to say to the life of the church today, especially to the ecumenical movement. We sometimes assume that the ultimate goal of Christian unity is to bring the various bodies of the church together into one organic institution. But the unity God wills for his people is more than ecclesiastical structure. Certainly communions who find themselves drawn together by a common heritage or compatibility in forms of work and worship should, for the sake of their effective witness, become organically one. But the unity of the church is more than merger. There may be disunity within a single church which is more sinful than the division of the church into denominations. Let us never assume that the problem of unity within the church is solved by merger. The union of denominations may become a blessed and useful means of expressing their essential oneness in Jesus Christ, but union witnesses to unity. It does not create it.

At the same time, it is possible for Christians in differing communions, who may worship according to different rights and forms, to be so closely bound together within the family of Christ because of their love for each other and their common allegiance to their Lord that they are truly members one of another within the Body. Here indeed is unity in diversity. The sin of our denominationalism is not that we call ourselves by different names within the body of Christ, but that through our differences, we have allowed ourselves to be separated in spirit one from the other. There is but one Lord, though he may be worshipped in different ways; one faith, though it may be expressed in different languages; and one baptism, though it may lead to many kinds of commitment (Eph. 4:5).

The unity of the church is in Christ himself. It is he who
212

draws us together. As members of the early church were bound to each other by their experiences of fellowship with their risen Lord, so in every age, it is in him that Christians find the meaning of their relationship to each other.

A few years ago, my wife and I were visiting the churches in Northern Nigeria in the heart of the African bush. On the first night of our visit, we were welcomed by a large and enthusiastic congregation, seated on mud brick pews, dressed in a way that seemed strange to us and speaking a language which we could not understand. Yet in spite of all our differences of race and culture, we immediately felt drawn together in a deep and meaningful fellowship. We were not really strangers to each other because we had a common friend, Jesus Christ. Indeed, he was more than a friend, he was our Lord. We belonged to each other because we all belong to him. The Nigerian pastor expressed our experience in his own picturesque language, "We have been brought together from different parts of the world like two pieces of cloth to be sewn together. And Jesus Christ is the needle."

God sends his Spirit upon a united church, made one not by organization or even by creed, but by the presence of the living Lord who draws all men unto him.

But note also that the disciples in the upper room while preparing themselves for their ministry devoted their time to *prayer* (Acts 1:14). They had received Christ's commission to witness to the world, but now they must wait for the power to fulfill that task. This could only come as they deepened their relationship with him their living Lord. So they continued in a ten-day prayer meeting.

Had some of us been among that little band, we certainly would have felt that this period of waiting was a sheer waste of time. With our passion for activity, we would feel that we should get on with the business of proclaiming the gospel. But we need to understand what they certainly knew, that before we can *do,* we must *be.* Before we can testify, we must experience.

For too many within the church, prayer has all but lost its meaning. We say our prayers to be sure, but there is too often little reality in them. They become simply a religious exercise instead of a genuine communion with God. Every great spiritual movement of the church has been born out of prayer. It was in a prayer meeting in Aldersgate Street in London that John Wesley found his heart strangely warmed, and out of which came the evangelistic revival in England and the United States. The most hopeful signs of spiritual renewal in the church today are having their origin in small prayer fellowships in churches all across the land. The gift of the Holy Spirit comes as an answer to prayer.

Prayer not only brings the Christian into constant fellowship with God; it keeps open the channels by which God's will is known to us. In the town of my childhood was an old mill turned by the power of a water wheel on a small stream. The millrace, however, would regularly be filled with leaves and twigs and other debris which would hinder the free flow of water through the huge wheel. It was necessary therefore that the channel be cleaned frequently or the mill would lose its power. Our lives, too, become cluttered with the debris of self interest and petty concerns. It is prayer which keeps open and clean the channel by which God's grace comes to us and through which his promised power is made available to all who will receive it. The first century Christians learned what the church of the twentieth century must also come to understand, that prayer is a prelude to the power of the Holy Spirit.

As we read the account of the pentecostal experience of the

214

early church, we cannot help but be impressed by the absolute seriousness with which these early Christians accepted their commission to be *witnesses* to the world. Out of their unity of spirit and fellowship of prayer was born a strength of purpose which changed the history of the world. The first disciples believed that unless the world came to receive Christ as Lord, it was lost. They were witnesses not only to what Christ had meant to them, but to what he must mean to all men everywhere. So they had a sense of urgency and expectancy out of which was born the power of their ministry.

One wonders, with all the resources of the church today, what would happen if Christians were willing to witness to the world with the same intensity of purpose, the zeal, and the recklessness which characterized the life of the early disciples. Halford Luccock has pointed out the words used by the various translations to describe the effect of Pentecost, "Astounded and bewildered, surprised and perplexed, amazed and astonished." Then he adds, "Let us ask ourselves—is our witness so clear, so unmistakable that we amaze anybody? Would any one of those six verbs ever be needed to describe the effect our church has on the surrounding community? If not, are we really in the Apostolic succession?"[1]

I knew a Sunday school superintendent who at the close of each church school session would always announce, "We will have church this morning as usual." Church as usual! Perhaps here has been our weakness. We have played at being the people of God without any real conviction that to us was entrusted the word that meant life or death for the whole world. When the church has lost its sense of urgency in witness, it has lost its power. Commitment and purpose are always prelude to power.

[1] *The First Fine Careless Rapture* (New York: Department of Evangelism of The National Council of Churches), p. 37.

I like to go to Orchestra Hall where I can hear the Chicago Symphony Orchestra. Before the concert, every musician is free to play any tune he chooses, in any key, at any tempo. The result is a kind of bedlam that is tolerated only because of what is to follow. This is freedom, yes, but it is not music. There is no real power in such disorder. Then the conductor steps to the podium and raps for silence—the symphony begins. The musicians are no longer free to play as they wish. Now they are under the direction of a great conductor. They all play the same composition in perfect rhythm, in the same key. What is the difference between the bedlam of the warm up and the beauty of the symphony? Each musician, now, whether playing the violin, the cello, the clarinet, or the bassoon, has a master. Each finds his true freedom in his surrender to him. All the skills of years of practice and discipline now suddenly find fulfillment in a glorious new harmony that is greater than the best that any one of the artists could offer alone. Here is the power of unity, disciplined relationship and purpose all expressed in a magnificent tribute to beauty under the will of the conductor. Let this be a parable of the church as we stand in this awesome moment of history.

Why should we assume that the gift of the Holy Spirit at Pentecost must be an isolated event in the history of the church? Surely God is waiting to pour out his Spirit upon all who will receive it at any age. But let the church today prepare for power even as the early church made ready to receive the gift of the Spirit. May the prayer of Harry Emerson Fosdick be answered with pentecostal fire:

> God of grace and God of glory,
> On thy people pour Thy power;
> Crown thine ancient church's story;

> Bring her bud to glorious flower.
> Grant us wisdom, grant us courage,
> For the facing of this hour. . . .[2]

[2] Used by permission of Harry Emerson Fosdick.

INTO ALL THE TRUTH

by ALVIN N. ROGNESS

President, Luther Theological Seminary,
St. Paul, Minn.

JOHN 16:12-15

When we confess, "I believe in the Holy Spirit . . . " we are in fact declaring that the triune God is still abroad among men.

When God had created the universe, he did not withdraw into some celestial rendezvous with himself and his holy angels and leave man to his own devices. When Jesus Christ had completed the work of man's redemption, neither did he ascend to heaven to recline in some padded throne at the right hand of the Father. He promised to be with us always, even to the end of the age. He assured his followers further, "But when your Advocate has come, whom I will send you from the Father— the Spirit of truth that issues from the Father—he will bear witness to me."

We are not left to an independent and lonely search for a God who has retreated from the scene of men. God himself, the Holy Spirit, is in ceaseless search of us. He broods in Word and Sacrament to call, gather, enlighten, sanctify, and preserve us for his heavenly kingdom.

The terrifying fact is that we can escape him. We can run

from him. He will pursue us to the end, but we can stay beyond his tender reach. When he calls, we can answer "no." Our judgment or punishment will be that we go through life and into eternity without him.

Whenever you hear his Word preached, whenever you read the Scriptures, whenever you come to the Lord's Supper, you have placed yourself within reach of this pulsating, pursuing presence of God. If you wish to stay beyond his reach, you should not risk the peril of being captured by him as he reaches out for you in the Word and Sacraments.

If, however, you want to be overtaken by him, let him approach you through these channels of grace. Your life will never be the same, but do you really want it to go on unchanged? Are there not longings and yearnings in your heart that you ardently hope might find fulfillment? Are there not fears and anxieties that you would like to have disappear? Are there not passions and appetites which you would gladly surrender to the command of Someone infinitely wiser than you?

To let God overtake you may not improve your skills in mathematics or astronomy. The truth into which he is eager to lead you is a truth which neither the telescope nor the microscope can reach. It is a truth about him and about you. It is a highly personal area of truth, so personal that it never leaves you as an impartial observer on the outside, looking in. You yourself are drawn into the truth as into a mighty and wonderful maelstrom. You become possessed of the truth, and the truth possesses you. The truth engulfs you and captures you.

Jesus of Nazareth was a strange man, so strange that even his early followers could not understand him as a man alone. When he asked his followers, ". . . who do you say I am?" Peter replied, "You are the Messiah, the Son of the living God" (Matthew 16:16). Three centuries later, the church had agreed

219

that he was indeed "God of God, Light of Light, Very God of Very God." Jesus was the incarnate One, Immanuel, God with us. Once and only once, in the long history of the human race, God had come to earth to be seen of men. And he had come, not merely to be seen, but by his life, death, and resurrection, to save the world from its sins. He had reopened the doors of the Father's great house to a lost and fallen world. In him and through him, we could return to the Father.

Jesus said, "I am the truth . . ." Other great teachers had said that they could show men the truth or lead them to the truth. Only Jesus had the divine audacity to lay claim to *be* the truth. A great teacher of mathematics, for instance, would be successful if he had led his students into the truth of mathematics. Jesus, the teacher, would be successful only if he succeeded in leading men to *himself,* who is the truth.

The role of the Holy Spirit, Jesus said, was to glorify Jesus— to lead men to him. No person can confess, "Jesus is Lord," except by the work of Someone from the outside. This Someone is the Holy Spirit. He is the divine, prodding agent to exalt Jesus and to usher men into his presence and fellowship.

Ushered into the presence of Jesus, you discover that the very first impulse which you have is to confess and to repent. You recognize instantly that you do not deserve to be in the same company with him. He is all holy; you are non-holy. And you know that it is not fitting for one who is not righteous and holy to comrade with one who is holy and righteous. With Isaiah you cry, "Woe is me . . . for I am a man with unclean lips." Or you recoil with Peter, "Depart from me, for I am a sinful man, O Lord." Or, better still, you plead with the publican. "Be merciful to me, a sinner."

You have come into the presence of Truth, and you cannot sit in the bleachers as an observer. You have become involved in God's way with you. You are a sinful being, in need of for-giveness. You need holiness and righteousness, if you are to re-main with him. And the Holy Spirit presents Jesus to you as the Savior. He is the Christ of the cross. You meet him there, at the foot of the cross. There you unburden your sins and guilt. He swallows them up in his unending mercy. Through faith in him, you receive his righteousness. Though your sins be as scarlet, in him they are white as snow. You rise up to walk with him in faith, a faith that takes hold of his promise of pardon, a faith that walks boldly into the Kingdom of God.

Confession of sin, repentance of sin, forgiveness of sin, and freedom to walk unshackled by sin—these are the gifts of the Spirit as he leads you into the presence of Jesus Christ.

But this is only the beginning. He will guide you into broader and deeper dimensions of the truth. He undertakes the task of making you over. He reshapes you, day by day, into the image of God. As a fellow-heir of Christ, you are to inherit the riches of God's Kingdom. You are to leave behind you the irksome cargo of your past and walk into a future charged with the splendor of God.

You now join the grand company of the disciples of Christ. You become a follower. Your pattern for life will now be the pattern which Christ chose for himself when he came to this earth. You are no longer a rival and competitor, you are now a neighbor and a brother. As Jesus came to be a servant of all, you now turn to become a servant of your neighbor. You may not like him, you may not even know him, but you are his servant nonetheless. And he is your brother.

This is the most radical change of all. The deep-seated ego-centricity which infects us all must now be shattered. We cannot walk with Christ and turn in upon ourselves, jealously guard-ing our rights and exploiting our advantages. We turn from ourselves to others. The rights of others, the feelings of others, the needs of others—these become now the center of our concerns. We reverse our course. And it is not easy.

The most stubborn stuff in this universe is not the granite in the mountains or the unchanging orbits of the wheeling stars. God has no trouble managing the myriad of bodies in his far-flung universe. But to change the stubborn stuff of the human heart required his death on a cross and the tireless working of the Holy Spirit. For the vindictive spirit of man to yield to the expansive spirit of love and forgiveness is a miracle of the first order. When a self-centered person turns to forget self in his concern for another, a tremor runs through the entire Kingdom of God. When a man lost in his sins is made to turn to God in repentance and faith and thus to become a part of the Kingdom, the angels of heaven break into applause. These are the miracles of the Holy Spirit.

These gigantic events, which excite the whole celestial company, may go quite unnoticed among men. The exploits of the Holy Spirit are not normally spectacular, measured by the standards of earth. A flight to the moon would instantly reach every headline in the world's press and send every television network agog. But when a man turns from darkness to light, when he leaves the enemy and returns to God, no one but God himself may know. But a mighty event has occurred, and a human life is on the path of a lifelong adventure and an eternity of wonder.

A child is brought to the Lord in holy baptism. He is grafted into Christ, as a branch is grafted into the trunk of a tree. He is ushered into the Kingdom. He is made a member of God's family. To the casual observer, nothing has happened except the celebration of an ancient Christian rite. But the command and promise of the Lord has made the simple use of water a

222

sacrament through which the Holy Spirit has quietly ushered a priceless soul into the Kingdom of God. Upon this event, the Spirit works throughout a lifetime to keep this child within the covenant of his baptism. If he falls away, his return will be a return to the life which was established with God through the sacrament.

If we but let him, the Holy Spirit will keep working within our hearts and minds to produce the kind of life which reflects the habits and the ways of the Kingdom. The signs or symptoms of the Holy Spirit's work, says Paul to the Galatians, are "love, joy, peace, patience, kindness, goodness, fidelity, gentleness, and self-control" (Galatians 5:22). These qualities may grow without fanfare, steadily and quietly, but they are the very qualities which give hope to the world. Without them, a man's life and the world's life would degenerate into meaninglessness, boredom, and futility. These qualities are the cement which holds all community life together. Man cannot be a brother to man without them.

These are the qualities, too, which make our unity in Christ a reality in daily living. Those who are baptized into Christ become a company commonly called the Christian church—the one, Holy, Christian and Apostolic Church. The church is not a company of people who like each other, who share the same skin or cultural values or who have agreed, as if in contract, to live and work together. The church is the company of those who are in Christ, all believers, regardless of their political, economic, racial, or cultural ties. If we are in Christ we have no option; we are one with one another. We belong to one another with a bond stronger and longer than any other tie on earth, for this union is the only one that extends beyond this life into the next.

The unity of all Christians is not something which we

choose; this unity is *given*. Our only escape from it is to escape Christ. We can treat this unity with indifference or even disdain, as we often have in the history of the church on earth. But the unity is there, nonetheless.

For a thousand years, and more especially in the last four hundred years, the various church bodies that have confessed the name of Christ have lived as if there were no unity. In the last fifty years, however, the Holy Spirit has used the events of history to force the churches of the Christian family to reassess their unity. Through the International Missionary Council and through the World Council of Churches, we have begun to regard one another as brothers in Christ, no matter what our denomination labels. More recently, through the great Vatican Council, the Roman Catholic church has re-examined itself and in so doing has turned its eyes to all those who have been baptized into Christ and are rediscovering them as brothers indeed. This mighty work of the Holy Spirit, awakening the followers of Christ to the unity that is theirs, must be a source of deep gratitude in the entire family of Christ.

A realized unity is probably more of a by-product of other fruits of the Spirit than an isolated achievement. When love and patience and kindness and fidelity are recovered among us, unity is the obvious result. These fruits are not given in a vacuum. They relate us to one another, under the tutelage of the Spirit of God.

It is not enough that this awakening finds expression in Geneva and Rome. It is our task to have this awakening grip the hearts and minds of people and congregations in one community after another. In any given village or city, the pastors and people of every Christian church will need to look upon one another as brothers and allies in one great enterprise, fighting under the one banner of Christ and against the foe and

224

foes common to all. With fidelity to the Truth, who is Christ, and guided by the Holy Scriptures, we are all under mandate to grow together and to edify one another. In his high priestly prayer, Jesus prayed to the Father: ". . . protect by the power of thy name those whom thou hast given me, that they may be one, as we are one. . . . But it is not for these alone that I pray, but for those also who through their words put their faith in me; may they all be one: as thou, Father, art in me, and I in thee, so also may they be in us . . . that they may be one . . . " (John 17). This prayer of Jesus seems to be more fulfilled in this century than it has been for many centuries. Within every congregation and among the congregations of the many communions, let us give the Holy Spirit his way with us, so that we may indeed become one.

There is no oneness in good will alone, however. Our oneness rests in Christ, the Truth. In faithfulness to the glorious gospel of his redemption and in this faithfulness alone can we hope to have the oneness which the Spirit gives. In love of his Word and in love of one another do we become what in Christ we are: one with one another.

The early centuries of the Christian church had their own glory. This century, too, can have a glory. Bewildered and dismayed as we are by the cataclysmic events of recent decades, we need not despair. God is still abroad. He may lead us to new insights and new heights, unparalleled in any other century. God's revelation in the Scriptures and in his Son is a mine not yet exhausted. The Spirit's power did not stop in the first century nor in the sixteenth. He keeps opening new doors, as Christ himself promised that he would. And who knows, we may be on the threshold of an era of unrivaled glory for our Lord?

225

TIME RIPE: TIME FULFILLED

by ELWYN A. SMITH

Pittsburgh Theological Seminary,
Pittsburgh, Pa.

The conviction that the church of Jesus Christ is an essentially unbroken body and that its present divisions ought to be healed is more than widespread; it is universal, for we must include with Christians who are ready to sacrifice something of their own traditon to unity the zealots who simply demand that everybody join them.

It is all the more sobering a reflection, in a period of high ecumenical enthusiasm, to recall that scarcely a dent has been made in the great three-fold division of Christendom between Orthodox, Catholic, and Protestant; that the total number of American Protestant bodies has not materially diminished; and that the prospect of Protestant unions like the Churches of Christ in Japan, the Philippines, Thailand, and South India is not good in the United States. Even though we are grateful for the power of this inward conviction that unity ought to come, must come, and will come, its weakness lies precisely in the fact that it is an imperative arising from human sources *within* the church. It draws strength from its timeliness but is endangered always by time itself, which eventually sweeps fashions of thought from the minds of men.

There are other forces, external and not subjective, that drive

226

the churches toward union. Small American denominations find it uneconomic to remain apart. They merge to save themselves. Mission boards are embarrassed by unseemly competition on the field and demand denominational co-operation. The world challenge of anti-Christianity, both communism and our own western preoccupation with things and things to do, drives Catholics and Protestants to ask themselves whether they can work effectively in alienation from each other. Secular history is generating powerful forces favorable to church unity.

With all these forces, both inward and outward, thrusting Christians toward one another, it is all the more depressing that we have accomplished so little. Perhaps the most significant form of modern church unity exists in the countries where Christians are outnumbered. Minority status has played an important role in the forming of the Churches of Christ in the Orient. If in these and other non-Christian cultures church unity appears an absolute necessity, it is still widely regarded in Europe and America as an option. "We are making out all right, we can wait," is an attitude widespread in official American church circles.

Against complacency, advocates of church union can bring nothing more effective than Scripture, theology, and appeals for renewal of evangelism. Is it only cynical to say flatly that in the face of the super-solvency of the elephantine American denominations, arguments from the Bible and Christian doctrine are all but futile? Steady shrinkage of membership lists, danger of bankruptcy, a risky clash with mainstream American opinion—these would be a different matter. They would actually threaten the churches. Mergers to save us would be quickly proposed. But Scripture, theology, and evangelism are not enough.

Even if a harmony of inner conviction and historical hardship were to give a new thrust to the trend toward union, what

227

assurance is there that its achievements would last? Movements wear themselves out. What would prevent the outbreak of another era of schism like the fifth century in the east, the sixteenth in the west, and the unbelievably fecund nineteenth in America? Those were times when "truth" was more important than unity, as the dividers put it. Maybe it is. Can the more complex view that truth and unity must be held together if either is to be valid in church life be sustained today?

The question we are raising comes to nothing less than this: in what does the unity of the church consist? On what does it depend for its formation and survival?

Let us give a direct answer. The unity of the church can never result from intense conviction and friendly historical conditions—that is, worldly hostility that forces us into union. It can only be produced and sustained by the divine action itself, by the miracle in which human beings are moved by God.

This, of course, is simon-pure preacher talk. Just this sort of religious phrasing ministers are expected to put out. They make their living with this special language and it belongs to them. Practical men know that if there is to be church union it must be planned and negotiated; it must be desired by a mass opinion that is not satisfied with things as they are. Practical men know how to negotiate. They can create mass sentiment through public relations techniques. They are not so arrogant as to claim to control the churches—if they did, church union could be achieved by resolving differences among leaders—but they know how such things are done and when they can be done. The real difference about church union among practical men is whether the time is ripe, which means that some think that union plans can be adopted and others that they cannot be. Both camps work hard to create public opinion which, upon appeal, will vindicate their judgment.

Practical men, of course, never attempt the impossible. They endanger their standing, even their identity, when they make errors of judgment. By all practical standards, then, a really adequate church unity is quite impossible for the present. For all the excitement created by John XXIII and Paul VI, is anyone ready to propose full reunion, to face the immense changes in both Catholicism and Protestantism that such a proposal would demand? The time is not ripe.

Eugene Carson Blake has proposed a daring and, in my opinion, a practicable move toward Protestant unity. Two things may be asked of it: is it the answer to Protestant disunity? Obviously not, since it is not inclusive—yet it could be a first step toward a really adequate Protestant reunion. Second, will it succeed? Methodism seems effectively to have withdrawn and most of the participating churches, at this writing, have barely enough popular support to keep them moving toward union. The time may be ripe or it may not be. If Methodists, Episcopalians, Presbyterians and the United Church of Christ cannot get together in the United States, what prospect is there for reunion in the face of the really deep chasms of Christian history, the break between Rome and the East, between Catholics and Protestants?

The rock in our love feast is just this—that Christian reunion is 99 per cent aspiration, it enlists far too few people, and neither the necessary depth of inward conviction nor the necessary harmony of historical circumstances exist to carry it much farther than it has gone. I hope for better things, but it is very possible that later historians will recognize that in the 1960's ecumenical enthusiasm crested, only to subside and await another tide in the affairs of men.

To such a sober suggestion there can be only one response: however truly church union may be an affair of men, it can

229

never rise solely on a tide in human affairs. If it is authentic, it is a response to the divine command and calling. Neither good nor bad judgment about whether the time is ripe, neither cosmopolitanism nor provincialism, theological nor Biblical arguments, neither smugness nor zeal will in the end be decisive, but only God's own action. If church union is an affair of men— history, conscience, negotiation, argument—it will never come to pass. But if it is an affair of God, it will succeed. This may occur in the midst of favorable historical circumstances, aroused consciences, effective argument, skilled negotiation. The resultant church will not be an ecclesiastical version of United Airlines but something freshly responsive to God, a community renewed by that newness of life granted us in Christ Jesus.

What does the ancient story of Pentecost teach but this? Before that miraculous gathering, marked by events which appear to modern readers to be purely mythological, the disciples were filled with hope and expectancy, aware of the high significance of Christ's reappearance among them, freed from the law and abounding in grace, constant in prayer and fellowship—but inert! The command to witness they either had not heard with the inward ear or, having heard it, had not the power to perform it.

Then came the gift of the Spirit—the imagery of the story is perfectly natural to the writer—and all was changed. This praying, aspiring, sharing fellowship got down to work. It did not achieve Christ's goals for it in the strength of its piety, favored by the religious fluidity of the Hellenistic age, nor in the intensity of its expectancy, nor with the aid of a persecuting state power that furnished it with martyrs. It succeeded simply in the power of the divine act and gift.

A historian's analytic method can demonstrate that the time was ripe for the conversion of the Mediterranean world to

Christianity. The Christian man, perhaps that same historian, will say that time was fulfilled. There is an infinite difference between the two. The ripeness of time bespeaks the natural process. Causes pile up and an effect cannot help but follow.

But the fullness of time is the moment that God himself chooses to bring history to focus and to manifest meaning in it. That was what happened in Christ and that was the power of Pentecost. Perhaps historical time was ripe for Christ; but in him God fulfilled his own "time." Perhaps at Pentecost the time was ripe for a spontaneous outburst of religious enthusiasm among the Christians suspended in hope; but it was God who acted there. He was uniquely responsible for the church's power to obey and to be.

The truths of Pentecost must be spoken in connection with the modern effort to achieve a renewal of common life among the church bodies that share the whole body of Christ. We do not know whether the time is ripe for an ultimate thrust toward full Christian reunion. We think not. We think an extended era of preparation is necessary and it is this era of preparing minds and wills that lies ahead of us. We do not hesitate to form such judgments because all men must, and to be impractical is not a virtue.

But we cannot stop here. Not only may we be wrong, but we may lack practical daring. The real question is not whether the time is ripe and whether we are capable of acting if it is; the critical question is whether we are faithful to God's action among us at this moment. If we are, union and much else will come. Christ's prayer for unity among his children is absolutely conclusive for faith. It admits of no casuistry.

Our disunity thus far and the poor prospect for any full reunion of Christians in our time is undeniable evidence that we have not been responsive to the whole divine action among

231

us. We have neither heard nor prayed the prayer of Christ. We have not believed that the time for the union of Christian hearts and church bodies is fulfilled but have preferred to speculate about when time would ripen.

The outcome of Pentecost is perhaps its most specific lesson. It puts Christian unity in perspective. The scene came to its climax with Peter's magnificent challenge: "This Jesus God raised up, and of that we are all witnesses. . . . Let all the house of Israel know assuredly that God has made him both Lord and Christ, this Jesus whom you crucified . . . ." (Acts 2:32, 36). The purpose of the gift of the Spirit, the total function of this intimate union of believers, was to put the fact of God's action in the world before men.

It is significant in our own time that Christian reunion has had its greatest success precisely where Christians are minorities which must witness or drown in seas of Hinduism, Buddhism, or secularism. Is the situation any different in Washington or New York, Chicago or St. Louis, Los Angeles or Dallas? Where the church will survive, it will witness; and where it will witness, it will be one. The church at Pentecost was above all a witnessing church. Church unity is not an end in itself. It is simply prerequisite to its duty of witness.

THE END OF THE BEGINNING

by RALPH W. SOCKMAN

Minister Emeritus, Christ Church, Methodist,
New York; Former Harry Emerson Fosdick
Visiting Professor, Union Theological Seminary,
New York

The Gospel of Luke and the Acts of the Apostles are generally considered to have been written by the same author. He begins the Acts with these words: "In the first book, O Theophilus, I have dealt with all that Jesus began to do and teach until the day when he was taken up."

Our minds go back to the Gospel record: the baptism of the young carpenter by John, the temptation in the wilderness, the telling of the matchless parables, the healing with its still unfathomed power, the period of popularity with applauding crowds, the turning toward Jerusalem and the cross, the "Triumphal Entry," the Last Supper, the tears in Gethsemane, the trial before Pilate, the crucifixion, the resurrection. It is, "the old, old story" and "those who know it best seem hungering and thirsting to hear it like the rest."

Yet to the author, all this was only what "Jesus began to do and teach."

Let us turn then to the last words which Luke records as spoken by Jesus before he was taken up: "And behold I send the promise of my Father upon you; but stay in the city until you are clothed with power from on high" (Luke 24:49).

233

Note first that Jesus left his earthly career with the *promise* of continuing divine power. Hear him elsewhere when he says: "I have yet many things to say to you but you cannot bear them now. When the Spirit of truth comes he will guide you into all the truth" (John 16:12-13). And again: "He who believes in me will also do the works that I do, and greater works than these will he do because I go to the Father" (John 14:12).

Our age of science is a journey into wonder. We wake up almost every morning exclaiming, "What will man do next?" But do we ever ask, "What will God do next?" The general impression seems to be that God, the First Cause, set this universe running by fixed laws and any new discoveries and inventions are due to man's manipulation of material forces.

Professor Paul Hoon of Union Theological Seminary tells of seeing a list of questions submitted to high school students for quick, off-the-cuff answers. One question was: "Do you think God understands radar?" They all answered, "No." Their feeling was that radar is a discovery made since God took his hands off.

Maybe we of the church are partly responsible for this popular impression. We speak of the gospel as "the faith once for all delivered to the saints." As a body of beliefs it is. The Bible contains all that is necessary to salvation. We do not need to add to its contents. But faith is also a living force as well as a corpus of doctrine. And it is capable of new development every day.

We say, "Jesus Christ, the same yesterday, today, and forever." He is. His historic personality is not subject to change. But electricity is the same yesterday, today, and forever. Its nature does not change. Yet electricity is a force with which we can do new things every day. So is it with Christ. He is a living force and he can take any one of us who is thoroughly com-

234

mitted to him and do things with us tomorrow whereby our religion would come alive in a new way.

In theological circles today much time is spent on exploring the records of the historical Christ. Bultmannism, demythologizing, linguistic analysis, and other phases of study seem very scientific to those in seminary circles. But to discuss the power of the living Christ and the potential of the Holy Spirit is so often regarded as beyond the pale of science in the realm of preaching, and as mere exhortation.

In 1955 the editors of *Fortune* magazine published *The Fabulous Future*. It was a symposium of eleven distinguished thinkers giving their views of America in 1980. The chapter on "War and Peace" was written by Robert E. Sherwood, the late great prize-winning playwright. In it he declared that if the "objective of disarmament is not achieved by 1980—long before 1980—then we may as well write FINIS to the human story." Then he went on: "All I can do is express the belief— or, if you will, the faith—that war will be a malodorous memory, existing only on the library shelves, and not on the front pages. If you ask me for convincing reasons for my optimism, I can provide no facts or figures, no blueprints, no statistics or charts or expert analyses. I can say only that my confidence in the future is founded on the fact that I believe in God. I believe in the assurance, given in the first chapter of the first book of the Bible, that 'God created man in his own image.' "[1]

I do not presume to fathom the mind of Sherwood, but his statement sets my mind running on this track. God is a creator and he made man in his own image to be a creator too. And God and man go on creating together. This means more than man's manipulation of material factors and forces to make

---

[1] Robert E. Sherwood, *The Fabulous Future* (New York: E. P. Dutton & Co., 1955), p. 149. Courtesy of *Fortune* Magazine, July, 1955.

new inventions and discoveries. This universe has mental and spiritual elements as well as material. God is a Father and we human beings are his children. Every father knows that if his son gets in proper response to him today, he can do new things with the lad tomorrow that he could not do yesterday. Likewise if we get in proper attunement with our heavenly Father, he can work greater things with us than he could yesterday.

There can be advance in the world of the spirit as in the world of space travel. Thus we can see why Jesus at his departure promised more truth to be revealed and greater things to be done by the Holy Spirit. The death and resurrection of Christ were but the end of the beginning.

We go on. When Jesus gave the Father's promise of power, he also gave the prescription: "Stay in the city until you are clothed with power from on high."

For one thing, the city of Jerusalem was the hard place for the disciples to stay. They might have returned to Galilee where Jesus had been popular. But Jerusalem was the city of their enemies, the center of tension, the place where stood the cross, the sign of their seeming defeat. The release of power from on high comes only to those who exercise their own power to the point of sacrifice.

This is a lesson we in our day need to learn. We have made a cult of the easy way. We measure our so-called progress by the increase of our comforts. Our houses are more luxurious, our hours of work are shorter, our means of travel more comfortable. Similarly we have tried to make our religious practices more painless. We move our churches nearer to our residences. We cushion the pews and air-condition the buildings. We seek to take the sting out of our pleas for church support by reminding the givers that their gifts are tax-exempt.

Now there is no value in needless drudgery and pain. But

236

there must be some point of sacrifice in our religion if it is to be effective. There was logic in the Old Testament practice of giving to the Lord the first of the harvest and the finest of the flock. It is the logic of love, felt by every mother when her child gives her the best apple in his bag. It is the principle experienced by the student at the piano when she keeps on struggling, "to get the hang" of her music until the music gets her. Only when we pass the point of no return to the easy way do we reach the point of great returns from God.

Jesus bade the disciples stay in the city, standing up to the hard situations until they could receive the power from on high.

Furthermore, by remaining in the city they would stay together. If the disciples had separated, their fervor would have evaporated. But they kept together for fellowship and food. They talked over their Lord's promises. They lived again their experiences of his love and power. They surrendered their wills to do their Lord's will as it should be revealed to them.

In a way, our contemporary church is making progress in getting together. The most significant advance in the Christian enterprise during the last half-century has been the growing ecumenical spirit. But underneath the surface there are some dangerously divisive tendencies. There are vocal and insidious forces attacking the National and World Councils of Churches and convincing multitudes that these great organizations are infiltrated by subversive elements. I have respect for those church members who are sincerely alarmed by the fear that the Christian churches are tainted with communism. But I have no respect for the professional patrioteers who have found how profitable it is to play on the fears and suspicions and hatreds of the masses. Nothing could please the communists more than to see the American churches divided into leftists and rightists.

237

If we are to be clothed with power from on high, we must keep together.

Moreover, Christ's prescription to stay in Jerusalem involved staying where the cross stood. That ugly reminder of their leader's death seemed the symbol of defeat. A few years later the deep-thinking apostle Paul would penetrate the truth and proclaim to the Corinthians: "We preach Christ crucified, a stumbling block to Jews and folly to Gentiles, but to those who are called, both Jews and Greeks, Christ the power of God and the wisdom of God" (1 Cor. 1:23-24).

But after nineteen centuries I wonder whether we of the church appreciate the power and wisdom of the cross. We talk about saving our metropolitan mass culture by getting at the power-structures of the city, meaning the political and financial and social leadership. Well and good. But not good enough unless we can prove and demonstrate the power of the cross. We keep repeating the prophet's words, "Not by might nor by power but by my spirit, saith the Lord." But we go on developing nuclear weapons and missile piles as the means for our protection. When the pulpit ventures to discuss racial integration, the pew often bids the preacher to stick to the gospel. And in sections where evangelists seem to have the most success in "leading souls to the cross," the racial barriers remain the most rigid.

Hear again Jesus' prescription for being clothed with power from on high. Stay in the city, the hard place which involved sacrifice. Stay in the city which meant keeping together. Stay in the city where stood the cross until the love revealed on it is realized to be the power of God and the wisdom of God.

And then came the power from on high at Pentecost when "they were all together in one place."

The receiving of "power from on high" seems mysterious and to some too nebulous for serious consideration. But it is the distinguishing work of man. Many have essayed to define what is the essential quality which differentiates man from the lower animals. Some have said that it is the power to think. But when I stood at the Seattle Exposition before the cage of the little apes and watched their clever antics, it was a bit hard for me to be sure that they were not thinking. And then when I looked around at some of the persons standing beside me, it was a bit hard for me to be sure that they were thinking!

Ernest Findlay Scott, the late great New Testament scholar, drew a better distinction between men and other animals when he declared that only man makes contact with a higher world, only man feels what we call inspiration. Have we not all experienced moments which "disturbed us with the joy of elevated thoughts" lifting us out of our leaden movements and dull routines? We cannot tell whence these higher thoughts come, but they give us new outlook and strength. That is "power from on high."

A daughter watched beside her mother's bed through weeks and months of illness. In the night hours as well as by day she waited and served. When it was over she exclaimed, "I didn't know it was in me to do all that." Maybe it wasn't in her own strength. She received power which was released from on high.

A composer with some achievements to his credit had fallen on hard times. Almost bankrupt in purse and half-paralyzed in body, he returned one night to his dismal lodgings in a drab section of London. He found there a manuscript with the request that he set it to music. He became so immersed in the task that he almost forgot to eat and sleep. And he came out with the great oratorio, *Messiah*. Later he told his friends that when he was composing the Hallelujah Chorus, he could hear angels singing and he only wrote down the music to which he was listening. Such is the power from on high.

John Wesley spent years trying to decide whether he would be a college teacher or a parish priest. He came to Georgia as a missionary to the colonists and Indians. He was not a success. Stirred by the sight of some Moravians who displayed a calm in the midst of a storm at sea, Wesley began seeking for inner power. One day he attended St. Paul's Cathedral in London and listened to an oratorio. Mellowed in spirit he went that night to a meeting in Aldersgate Street. There, while a layman was reading, Wesley felt his "heart strangely warmed." Conscious of "that power from on high," he went out to change the moral climate of England.

A wise observer of our time recently wrote that wherever we look we find able men doing good work, but we miss all signs of inspiration, and that perhaps our chief need in these modern days is to recover that old belief in the (Holy) Spirit.

Aye, and aye again! Christ gave the promise and the prescription. God gave the power at Pentecost. And the Spirit still speaks: "Behold, I stand at the door and knock; if any one hears my voice and opens the door, I will come in to him and eat with him and he with me."

PRAYER AND THE HOLY SPIRIT*

by W. A. VISSER 'T HOOFT

General Secretary, World Council of
Churches, Geneva, Switzerland

"And when they had prayed, the place in which
they were gathered together was shaken; and they
were all filled with the Holy Spirit and spoke the
word of God with boldness."

—ACTS 4:31

The very young church in Jerusalem is in the midst of its
first conflict with the world. Its immediate reaction is to pray.
God answers that prayer by filling the church with the Holy
Spirit.

But was that prayer not superfluous? Had the church not
already been filled with the Holy Spirit on the day of Pentecost? Had Peter and John and their friends in the little Jerusalem congregation not been present when the tongues of fires
appeared and rested on each of them?

The answer is surely that the church and therefore every
single member of the church can only be filled with the Spirit
by continuing to *pray* for the gift of the Spirit. For the Spirit is
present in the manner of a personal relationship, not in the

* A sermon preached during the 19th General Council of the World Alliance
of Reformed Churches which met Aug. 3–13, 1964, at Frankfurt Main,
Germany.

manner of a force which can be appropriated once for all. Calvin speaks clearly on this point: "It is not that the grace of the Holy Spirit is perpetually bound up with the word of men. . . . The servants of God with their planting and watering do nothing at all, unless the growth comes from the secret efficacy of the Spirit." It is a profound delusion to conceive the Spirit, as was done by Simon of Samaria, in such a way that it is possible to *own* the Holy Spirit and to use it as one of the most useful in a collection of magical tricks.

Because the Holy Spirit is *personal,* we can only be in relation with him, if we stand in the attitude of readiness for personal encounter with him. To use modern terminology: the I-Thou relation is fundamentally different from the I-it relation. I can deal with an "it" as my possession. But if I seek to do the same with a "Thou" I break off the relationship at the very outset. There can only be a true intrapersonal meeting, if the I and the Thou have a true desire for such meeting and have respect for each other as persons. Now the Spirit is a person in the divine Trinity. How then can I ever meet the Spirit unless I speak to him in the only way I can address God, that is by *prayer?*

It is therefore deeply meaningful that this Assembly, which would help the churches to understand more deeply the biblical teaching about the Holy Spirit and to live by the grace and force of the Spirit, has as its central theme the prayer for the Holy Spirit. If this Assembly will do just one single thing, namely, to make us all deeply aware how desperately we need the Holy Spirit, we will not have come to Frankfurt in vain.

But to pray for the Holy Spirit is also a risky thing. We need not worry about the reaction which will certainly come: "Why are these Christians always *asking* for the Holy Spirit. Don't they ever *get* it?" For that is again based on the wrong notion that you can receive the Spirit without praying for it. But we should worry about the *real* question, whether we mean with heart and soul what we say we mean and whether we are ready to take the consequences. "Veni, Creator Spiritus" cannot possibly be taken to signify: "Let's have a little bit of Holy Spirit; just enough to put some more energy into our often sleepy ecclesiastical institutions." It can only mean: "Come, Thou living God, Thou living Christ and Thou Creator Spirit, Giver of Life, transform us altogether, so that we may be truly converted, radically changed."

Our text speaks of the consequences: "The place in which they gathered together was shaken." When the Holy Spirit appears on the scene our human structures are subjected to a severe shock treatment. It is not that everything is destroyed, but rather as we read in Hebrews 12: "the removal of what is shaken, as of what has been made, in order that what cannot be shaken may remain." It is the operation by which everything is taken away that is not essential for the life of the church. It is the reopening of the source which had become obstructed and could not flow unhindered. It is that renewal in the Holy Spirit or by the Holy Spirit which, according to the epistle to Titus, we owe to the goodness of our Saviour-God.

We know something about this kind of earthquake. For we are the children of a Reformation which we can only understand as a mighty intervention of the Holy Spirit in the life of the church. We admit that from the human point of view that spiritual earthquake destroyed much that seemed respectable and worthy of admiration. But we believe, do we not, that at that time, as in all times, the one decisive consideration had to be: How can the Holy Spirit again take hold of the church? That question could only be answered by a great concentration on the one thing needful, a repudiation of false accretions, of distortions, of the non-essential. For as Luther said: "The Holy Spirit knows only how to preach Christ; the poor Holy Spirit knows nothing else."

It would seem that in our time the Spirit is again shaking the place in which the church finds itself. In fact we are in the midst of two earthquakes: The one which has its epicenter in the world, the other which has its epicenter in the church.

Do we recognize their significance? As so many seemingly strong positions which the Christian church once occupied in the field of civilization are breaking down, as the church in so many parts of the world is being thrown back upon that pristine, nude existence in which it has nothing else to offer except the bare gospel, as many Christians now have to pay a heavy price for their confession and witness, we are inclined to regret the fleshpots of the time when the church shaped the whole life of the nations and we get deeply worried about its future. But could it not be that this is the shaking of the churchly edifice, the action of cleansing by the Holy Spirit, which must precede the coming of the Holy Spirit in power? Is it perhaps that the earthen vessels have too much obscured the treasure and that they must therefore be replaced by less imposing instruments?

There is also the earthquake in the life of the churches themselves: the calling in question of all our traditions and institutions; the way in which through the ecumenical movement all of us are challenged to redefine what we really believe; the unprecedented and unexpected encounter with the Roman Catholic church which suddenly shows possibilities of a real renewal; the challenges that come from the younger churches. Are we to become nervous about the vast insecurity of our present situation and the great uncertainty concerning the future? Or are we to say: It might be that this great shaking

244

of the foundation is a sign that the Holy Spirit is preparing a new day and that we are to watch for the signs of his coming.

In recent years we have all spoken much about renewal of the church. But have we realized that renewal can only be renewal *by the Holy Spirit?* Are not many of our congregations in the situation of the disciples of John who have heard of the Spirit? Do not such persons take the attitude that they cannot speak to the Spirit because you do not speak to people unless you have been personally introduced to them? And is this not the reason why there are many more people in the world who think of Christians as people who smoke opium rather than as people filled with new wine?

The result of the coming of the Spirit is that the young church speaks the word of God with boldness. That seems at first a rather obvious consequence. We might even think that we are in step with the early church, if we send enough resolutions to our governments and don't allow anyone to curtail the rights and privileges of our churches. But that is not what this particular boldness means at all. This "parresia" for which few of our languages have a truly adequate synonym and which is perhaps best rendered in the German "Freimut," has deeper and wider dimensions.

It has first of all to do with our approach to God. The Holy Spirit gives us the courage to go to him, to overcome our false complexes of fear, or complacency, or despair and to say: "Abba, Father." When St. Paul in II Corinthians 3 characterises the difference between the old and the new dispensation, he says that we now live in the dispensation of the Spirit, that therefore we may have much parresia, that is, much courage or confidence in our approach to God, and may behold his glory with unveiled face. And he repeats that this comes from the Lord, the Spirit (II Cor. 3:12-18).

The same truth is beautifully expressed in that central part of the ancient liturgy of St. John Chrysostom, used by the Eastern Orthodox Churches, where the *Epiklesis,* the invocation of the Holy Spirit, takes place. Such a prayer to the Holy Spirit at the decisive moment of the communion service ought really to find its place in every Christian liturgy. For it asks for the coming down of the Holy Spirit so that the communion may be "for the parresia, the boldness to approach Thee neither unto judgment nor unto condemnation."

When the Holy Spirit has removed the wall between God and ourselves, when we are at the point that we do not only know *about* God, but live before his face and in conversation with him, then the other boldness, the boldness in our witness to all men, follows naturally. Then we are sent out to the world. Pentecost means the birth of the witnessing, missionary church. It is the Holy Spirit who is the true actor in the dramatic developments recorded in the book of Acts. It is the Spirit which has made men in all times and places confessors and evangelists and martyrs. No one can proclaim the lordship of Christ in all the world and over all the world except by the Holy Spirit. So if that true boldness is lacking, if our congregations do not have the missionary zeal, if we ourselves are hesitant in our evangelism, the sickness can be clearly identified: we are not truly familiar with the Holy Spirit, and the only remedy is to turn to him, to long for him, to pray to him.

We have good reason to worry as we do about the communicating of the gospel to a rapidly changing world. But that must never become our deepest concern. The primary question is whether we *have* a living gospel to preach, whether we have the word of divine authority which only the Holy Spirit can give us.

We meet in the place where a new departure was made in
246

the confessing of the faith. For it was here in Frankfurt that Karl Barth wrote down the Barmen Declaration which gave the confessing church in Germany its word of true parresia, its clear testimony to the unique lordship of Christ over against the syncretism of Christianity with a pagan ideology. In that declaration we find the simple and clear words: "The Christian Church is the community of brethren in which Jesus Christ acts presently in Word and Sacrament by the Holy Spirit. . . . We reject the false doctrine that the Church is permitted to form its message or its order according to its own desire or according to prevailing philosophical or political convictions."

We know what a profound effect that declaration had on the life of the church in Germany and in other countries. But we think too easily that such confession belongs only to times of exceptional crisis in church history. Are we not constantly faced with the opportunity and necessity to speak out clearly over against all the syncretisms of our time, the mixing of the gospel with nationalism or racialism or power-politics, or the easy adaptations of the gospel to the modern world in which the great deeds of God and, above all, the central events of the incarnation and the resurrection are obscured? Luther has said: "The Holy Spirit does not sit on the fence."

To the world around us the theme of our meeting may seem to be one more proof that the churches are always looking inward and dealing with their own private concerns which are incomprehensible to the world. I have already heard it said that this theme of the Holy Spirit is so esoteric, so far away from the problems of ordinary men and women in the technical society of the 1960's, that it is almost impossible to arouse any interest for it. Are we able to answer this challenge?

If we spend our time in Frankfurt in what may be for ourselves fascinating theological discussions about the Holy Spirit, we will have demonstrated that the world is right. But if we not only talk about the prayer to the Holy Spirit, but actually live together by the strength and in the light of that prayer, then we will have an answer for the world. For then the Spirit will send us into the world with that which the world most needs. Then it will have been a rediscovery of the one source of true renewal, of rejuvenation, yes, or resurrection, which can bring healing to a decaying Christendom and a disintegrating society. Then, being set on our feet by the Holy Spirit, we will have the nerve to tackle the thorny problems of our time and stand up for justice to those who suffer under racial or social or ideological oppression, or speak the word of reconciliation in the midst of the great conflicts of our day.

In closing I would summarise a passage from one of the earliest addresses of Dietrich Bonhoeffer, given at an ecumenical youth conference in 1932:

"The faithless world says: The Church is dead. Let us celebrate its funeral.

The faithless world, which still has pious illusions, says: The Church is not dead, it is only weak. Let us serve it with all our strength and help it to thrive.

The faithful say: The Church lives in the midst of dying, only because God calls it from death to life and, does the impossible through us, in spite of us."

If Bonhoeffer is right, as I believe he is, the prayer to the Holy Spirit, the Giver of Life, is a matter of life and death for us all.

Type, 11 on 13 and 10 on 11 Garamond
Display, Futura
Paper, Spring Grove E.F.